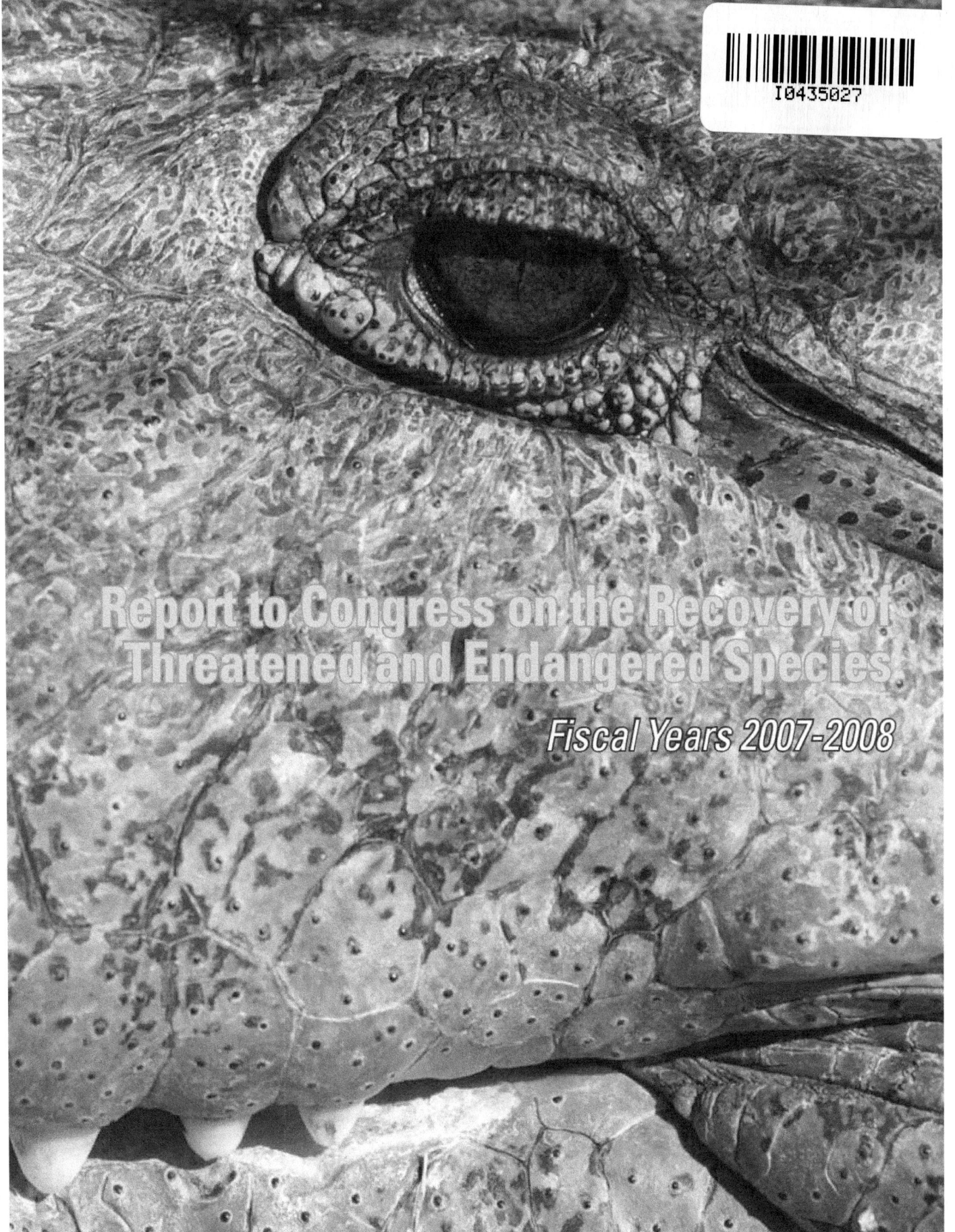

U.S. Fish & Wildlife Service

I0435027

Report to Congress on the Recovery of Threatened and Endangered Species

Fiscal Years 2007-2008

From the Director

The ultimate goal of the Endangered Species Act (Act) is recovery of threatened and endangered species. Recovery is the process by which the decline of threatened and endangered species is arrested and threats are removed or reduced so that long-term survival of the species can be maintained in the wild, thus alleviating the need for the protections of the Act. As of September 30, 2008, the U.S Fish and Wildlife Service (Service) had lead responsibility for recovering 1,268 federally listed threatened (280) and endangered (988) species.

The purpose of this Recovery Report to Congress is to provide an update on the recovery of listed species for Fiscal Years 2007-2008. During this time, recovery has been achieved for three species. The Service has delisted the Yellowstone distinct population segment (DPS) of the grizzly bear, the bald eagle (except in Arizona), and the West Virginia northern flying squirrel. In addition, the Florida DPS of the American crocodile has been downlisted and six other species have been proposed for delisting. The polar bear and Sonoran Desert DPS of the bald eagle (in Arizona) were added to the Federal List of Threatened and Endangered Wildlife and Plants.

As part of this Recovery Report, updates on recovery plan information are given. Recovery plans define goals for downlisting and delisting by making recommendations for specific conservation measures. The Service has demonstrated a marked improvement in finalizing recovery plans for threatened and endangered species. By the end of this reporting period, 1,087 species (85%) had final recovery plans, which is a three percent increase from two years ago. In addition, 47 more species had draft plans that were waiting to be finalized.

Because species' declines often occur over the course of decades or centuries prior to their listing, recovery often requires substantial time and resources to achieve. By conducting 5-year status reviews, the Service can determine how much progress is being made towards recovery. These reviews also help us determine whether a species should be delisted or reclassified. In the past, the Service had not regularly conducted 5-year status reviews because of other competing statutory requirements. However, recent lawsuits and notices of intent to sue have highlighted the need to undertake 5-year status reviews. The Service's Washington Office has recommended that each region complete 20% of its species' 5-year status reviews annually. So far, 887 or 70% of all listed species have had 5-year status reviews initiated, and of those initiated, 329 or 37% have been completed. Of the 329 completed 5-year status reviews, 285 (87%) recommended no change in status for the species, 23 recommended downlisting, 18 recommended delisting, and only 3 recommended uplisting from threatened to endangered.

This Recovery Report also provides information on overall species' status relative to the previous reporting period. These results are not intended to provide status review results such as are available after a 12-month petition finding or a 5-year status review. They are intended only to represent the relative progress that is being made on listed species. By the end of this reporting period, 551 species or 43% were considered stable or improving. However, there were 389 species whose status was decreasing (30%), 301 species' status was unknown (24%), and 19 species were presumed extinct (1%).

Recovering species that are threatened with or in danger of becoming extinct is a daunting task. The Service cannot accomplish this alone. We must rely on Federal, State, local agencies, Tribes, non-governmental organizations, universities, private landowners, and other stakeholders for their help. We recognize that the authorities, resources, and cooperation of all of our partners will be required to achieve recovery of threatened and endangered species.

Rowan W. Gould, Acting Director

This page intentionally left blank.

Report to Congress on the Recovery of Threatened and Endangered Species
Fiscal Years 2007-2008

Data

Data are presented for each U.S. listed species under the jurisdiction of the U.S. Fish and Wildlife Service (Service), organized by major taxonomic groupings. Data include:

- the species' inverted common name, or scientific name where no common name is available;
- the lead Service Region;
- the date the species was listed under the Act;
- the date of the species' first final recovery plan (if there is one);
- the stage of development of the recovery plan;
- the date of the species' most current recovery plan;
- the species' current listing classification;
- the species' recovery priority number;
- the date the species' 5-year review was initiated;
- the date the species' 5-year review was completed;
- the species' population status at the end of FY 2008;
- the number of actions outlined in the current recovery plan that have been implemented;
- the estimated costs for recovery, if available; and
- the estimated time to recovery (from plan completion), if available.

Common Name

Species are listed in the table by inverted common name within their respective taxonomic groups. Where a species has more than one commonly accepted common name, the alternate name is indicated in parentheses with an "equals"

symbol followed by the alternate name. The scientific name is also given in parentheses behind the common name. Many plants and some invertebrates have no common name, so only the scientific name is given.

Lead Region

This indicates which Service Region has the lead responsibility for the species (see Map on inside back cover). For example, a number "8" indicates a species for which the California-Nevada Regional Office has lead responsibility. Some species are wide ranging and may be found in more than one region.

Date Listed

This indicates the date the species was added to the list of federally Endangered and Threatened Species.

Date of First Final Plan

This indicates the date that the first final recovery plan was ap-

The city of Yreka, California, is a partner with the Fish and Wildlife Service in efforts to recover the Yreka phlox, an endangered wildflower.

Matt Braun/FWS

proved (signed by the Regional Director or Director). An N/A in this column indicates that the species does not yet have a final recovery plan.

Plan Status

The status of recovery plan development is reported as indicated below:

- F = Final plan has been approved by the Regional Director and a Notice of Availability has been published in the Federal Register.
- D = Draft plan has been approved by the Regional Director and published in the Federal Register as available for public comment.
- RD(#) = Draft of the revised plan has been approved by the Regional Director and published in the Federal Register as available for public comment. The draft of the first revision to the final plan is recorded as RD(1), draft of the second revision to the final plan is recorded as RD(2), etc.
- RF(#) = Final revision has been approved by the Regional Director and a Notice of Availability has been published in the Federal Register. The first revision is recorded as RF(1), the second revision is RF(2), etc.
- E = Species that are exempted from recovery plan development. Species are "exempt" if the Service has determined that developing a recovery plan will not promote the conservation of the species.
- N/A = the species does not yet have an approved recovery plan.

Date of Current or Active Plan

This indicates the date of the species' most current recovery plan. An "N/A" in this column indicates that a recovery plan for the species is still under development. A date in this column that is different from the date in the Date of First Final Plan column indicates that the plan has undergone a revision (or is currently undergoing a revision) or that earlier drafts and final plans for some individual species may have been incorporated into later multi-species or ecosystem plans.

Listing Classification

The species' listing classification, as of September 30, 2008, is identified as threatened (T) or endangered (E).

Recovery Priority Number

The first step for the conservation of any species is to prevent its extinction. Thus the species with the highest degree of threat have the highest priority for preparing and implementing recovery plans.

Additionally, appropriate use of the limited resources available to implement the Act, must be considered. To this end, each species is assigned a recovery priority from 1 to 18 according to the degree of threats, recovery potential, and taxonomic distinctness. In addition, a species' rank may be elevated by adding a "C" designation to its numerical rank to indicate that it is, or may be, in conflict with construction or other development projects, or other forms of economic activity. Species with a high priority rank (1, 1C, 2, 2C) are those that are the most threatened and have the highest potential for recovery. Species with a low rank (16, 17, 18) are the least threatened and have low recovery potentials. See 48 FR 43098-43105 (Sept. 21, 1983), and Table 3 on 48 FR 51935 (Nov. 15, 1983) for additional information on this prioritization system.

Although Recovery Priority Numbers are intended to serve as guidelines for prioritizing development and implementation of recovery plans, many other factors affect how we allocate limited recovery resources. The Service allocates the majority of its general recovery funding to the Regional Offices through a methodology that uses the number of species and the likely complexity of recovery, for instance a wide-ranging animal species would be weighted higher (and receive more funding) than an endemic plant. Individual regions and field offices prioritize funding for listed species based on a variety of other factors that likely include the species recovery priority rankings, degree of threat, and potential for success. However, many other factors affect how we allocate our limited recovery funding. These other factors include the number of species benefitting from an action, partnership opportunities, leveraging of funding with other partners, whether the action will benefit other species, and whether the action will promote recovery or improve species status over a large geographic area. In addition, some recovery funding is necessarily expended to maintain a species status or move a species closer to recovery and delisting. As a species moves closer towards achieving recovery, the degree of threats to the species decreases, and is reflected in a lower RPN. However, without continued funding for ongoing or remaining recovery actions, it is often impossible to maintain a species' improved status or to delist the species. Therefore, some funding decisions are made based on the need to maintain a species' improved status, on the ability to move a species closer to recovery, or to move a species to the point that it is fully recovered and ready for delisting.

Relying more on RPNs as a factor in allocating recovery funding is challenging due to the difficulty in keeping RPNs up to date to reflect the species' current status under

The Palos Verde blue butterfly of southern California benefits from captive-rearing facilities set up to recover this endangered species.

© Moose Peterson/Wildlife Research Photography

changing threat conditions. In some cases, it may even be difficult to assess whether changing conditions warrant a change in RPNs. For example, the Indiana bat, gray bat, and Virginian big-eared bat have RPNs of 8, 8, and 9C, respectively (indicating species with moderate threats and high recovery potential). However, the appearance of the disease "white-nose syndrome" in the Northeastern U.S. poses a potentially deadly threat to all bat species. The degree of threat is unknown but could potentially be very high. The ability to protect bat species from or remove the threat of white-nose syndrome (recovery potential) is also unknown, making it difficult to determine an appropriate RPN based on degree of threat and recovery potential. The Service moved forward to fund proposals to investigate the causes and monitor the extent of the disease over funding actions for species that have higher RPNs. In this case, the Service needed to respond quickly to a potentially grave threat before knowing enough to positively quantify it in a changed RPN. Additionally, swift actions to monitor and prevent spread of the disease are likely needed to prevent recovery potential of these species from moving from high to low. As we describe below, we are implementing several measures to ensure that RPNs are periodically reviewed and updated and expect to examine the RPNs of our listed bat species through this process.

While the Service's RPN guidelines are intended to be used as a guide for prioritizing recovery planning and implementation rather than being an inflexible framework, we have undertaken several steps to ensure that RPNs are regularly reviewed and updated. These changes will help RPNs keep pace with the on-the-ground conditions for our listed species, and increase their relevance in decision-making. We have implemented yearly review of RPNs during our annual performance reporting, and included review of RPNs as part of our periodic species 5-year reviews required by section 4(c)(2) of the Act. Currently, changes in RPNs can only be entered once a year in the Service's TESS (Threatened and Endangered Species System) database during our annual performance reporting. We are developing mechanisms in TESS that will allow us to update RPNs as needed throughout the year so that the RPN displayed in the Service's databases won't lag behind the actual species' condition. This change will also allow us to display accurate RPNs on the species profiles posted on our Endangered Species public website, and to better communicate our recovery priorities to our partners and stakeholders.

Fish and Wildlife Service biologist Judy Jacobs feeds a young Laysan albatross at Kilauea Point National Wildlife Refuge in Hawaii, as part of research into methods to translocate the endangered short-tailed albatross.

Brenda Zaun/FWS

Fish and Wildlife Service staff net Rio Grande silvery minnows brought by truck from New Mexico to reestablish the species at Big Bend National Park in Texas. Volunteers and partners in the program passed buckets of the fish down the line to a temporary pen in the river prior to release.

Five-year Status Reviews

The information displayed represents the five-year status reviews currently defined for the species. The initiation date is the date a notice was published in the Federal Register which announced the initiation of the five-year status review and requested any new information relevant to the species. The completion date is the date the five-year status review was signed by the Service's Regional Director or appropriate delegated authority.

Species Status (FY 2008)

The population status of each species is identified as:

- Improving: Species for which information available indicates that the species status improved since the last reporting period (i.e. population numbers increased, threats decreased or were managed, or both).
- Stable: Species for which the information available indicates that the species status neither improved nor declined since the last reporting period (i.e., population numbers remained constant, and threats did not affect species status during reporting period).
- Declining: Species for which the information available indicates that the species status declined since the last reporting period (i.e., population numbers decreased, threats increased or continued to impact the species, or both).
- Uncertain: Species for which the information available is not sufficient to determine their status since the last reporting period (i.e. significant level of uncertainty in effects of threats, or significant and/or extended lack of information on population numbers or other demographic characteristics over most or all the species range).
- Captivity: Species that are found only in captivity, and not in the wild within its range.
- Presumed Extinct: Species that are believed to be extinct, but may not be confirmed so, or species for which surveys have been conducted to confirm extinction, but are awaiting completion of the delisting rule.
- Presumed Extirpated in the U.S. and Extant outside the U.S.: Cross-border species believed or confirmed to no longer exist in the U.S., but still occur elsewhere within its range outside the U.S.

Number of Actions Implemented

The "number of actions implemented" represents the total number of recovery actions identified in the implementation schedules of the recovery documents in the Recovery Online Activity Reporting (ROAR) database that have been implemented. Recovery Actions are defined as actions

Rio Grande silvery minnow.

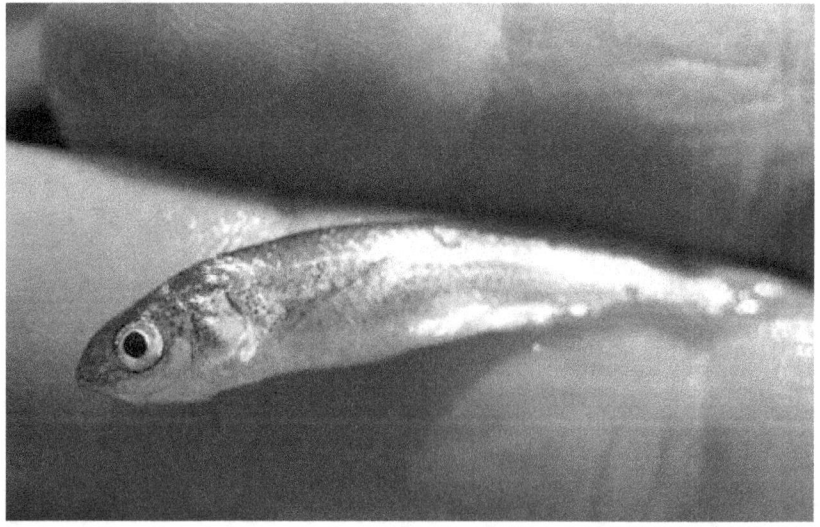

relevant to eliminating or reducing the threats identified in listing rules, recovery plans, and through subsequent 5-year reviews that are identified as such in ROAR. A recovery action in ROAR will count as "implemented" if it has an action status of ongoing current, ongoing not current, partially complete, or complete (if it has an associated completion date within the current FY). Caution needs to be applied when reviewing the total number of recovery actions implemented. Many species are included in multi-species recovery plans so some actions may be listed more than once. These data represent the number of actions implemented in FY 2008 only. Prior to FY 2008 we only collected data on the number of actions initiated for which the Service was identified as the lead or co-lead in the implementation schedule.

The "number of actions implemented" replaces the "recovery achieved" data that we have included in previous Recovery Reports to Congress. For recovery achieved, we reported a value of 1 to 4 that corresponded with a percentage of the species recovery objectives that had been achieved. However, this number did not necessarily correspond with the percentage of recovery actions implemented and we found that it was difficult to ensure that the measure was being applied consistently for all listed species. With the development and widespread use of the ROAR database, we now have an efficient means of tracking the actual number of recovery actions implemented. We believe that this value serves as a better indicator of the level of effort being invested to recover each listed species. We first began collecting these data in FY 2008 as we implemented reporting on the performance measures identified in the Endangered Species Program's draft strategic plan.

An endangered black-footed ferret gains its freedom at a reintroduction site in Kansas.

Dan Mulhern/FWS

Estimated Costs for Recovery

This column indicates the estimated costs of recovering the species as reported in their most current final recovery plans. In many cases, this estimate is a minimum estimate because many plans include recovery actions for which the costs are yet to be determined. Multi-species plans often only report an estimated cost for recovery for all species in the plan, thus a single action might benefit multiple species simultaneously. In these cases, the total cost provided in the multi-species plan has been associated with every species from the plan. Cost estimates are not adjusted for inflation, but are relevant to the year the plan was completed.

Estimated Time to Recovery

This reports the estimated number of years (from the date of the current plan) the recovery plan forecasts it will take the species to recover in order to begin delisting. All time estimates are based on the assumption that adequate resources are available to implement all recovery actions identified as necessary for the recovery of the species in a timely fashion. Data are reported only for those recovery plans which provide an estimate of time to delisting. An "N/A" in this column indicates that the recovery plan only reports the time estimated to reclassification, not delisting, or that the time to delisting is expected to be determined at some later date.

Recovery Data as of September 30, 2008

GENERAL SPECIES INFORMATION					RECOVERY PLAN INFORMATION						SPECIES/RECOVERY STATUS		
Species Name	Lead Region	Date Listed	Date of First Final Plan	Plan Status*	Date of Current or Active Plan	Number of Actions Implemented	Estimated Costs for Recovery	Estimated Time to Recovery (years)	Listing Classification	Recovery Priority Number	FY 2008 Species' Status	Date 5-Year Status Review Initiated	Date 5-Year Status Review Completed
Amphibians													
Coqui, golden (Eleutherodactylus jasperi)	4	11/11/1977	4/19/1984	F	4/19/1984	6	N/A	N/A	T	5C	Presumed Extinct	9/27/2006	N/A
Frog, California red-legged (Rana aurora draytonii)	8	5/23/1996	5/28/2002	F	5/28/2002	104	N/A	N/A	T	6C	Unknown	N/A	N/A
Frog, Chiricahua leopard (Rana chiricahuensis)	2	6/13/2002	6/4/2007	F	6/4/2007	78	3,413,000	28	T	2C	Improving	5/2/2007	N/A
Frog, Mississippi gopher (Rana capito sevosa)	4	12/4/2001	N/A	N/A	N/A	N/A	N/A	N/A	E	5	Decreasing	N/A	N/A
Frog, mountain yellow-legged (Rana muscosa)	8	7/2/2002	N/A	N/A	N/A	N/A	N/A	N/A	E	3	Stable	N/A	N/A
Guajon (Eleutherodactylus cooki)	4	6/11/1997	9/24/2004	F	9/24/2004	22	846,000	20	T	11	Stable	9/12/2005	N/A
Salamander, Barton Springs (Eurycea sosonum)	2	4/30/1997	9/21/2005	F	9/21/2005	48	6,255,000	20	E	2C	Improving	1/25/2005	10/5/2006
Salamander, California (Santa Barbara County DPS) (Ambystoma californiense)	8	1/19/2000	N/A	N/A	N/A	N/A	N/A	N/A	E	3C	Decreasing	4/24/2007	N/A
Salamander, California tiger (Sonoma County DPS) (Ambystoma californiense)	8	7/22/2002	N/A	N/A	N/A	N/A	N/A	N/A	E	3C	Stable	N/A	N/A
Salamander, California tiger (Central CA DPS) (Ambystoma californiense)	8	8/4/2004	N/A	N/A	N/A	N/A	N/A	N/A	T	9C	Decreasing	N/A	N/A
Salamander, Cheat Mountain (Plethodon nettingi)	5	8/18/1989	7/25/1991	F	7/25/1991	23	N/A	N/A	T	8C	Stable	12/16/2008	N/A
Salamander, desert slender (Batrachoseps aridus)	8	6/4/1973	8/12/1982	F	8/12/1982	37	N/A	N/A	E	8	Stable	2/14/2007	N/A
Salamander, flatwoods (Ambystoma cingulatum)	4	4/1/1999	N/A	N/A	N/A	N/A	N/A	N/A	T	5	Decreasing	6/14/2005	N/A
Salamander, Red Hills (Phaeognathus hubrichi i)	4	1/3/1977	11/23/1983	F	11/23/1983	9	N/A	N/A	T	7	Unknown	9/8/2006	N/A
Salamander, San Marcos (Eurycea nana)	2	7/14/1980	4/8/1985	RF(1)	2/14/1996	36	N/A	N/A	T	2C	Stable	3/20/2008	N/A
Salamander, Santa Cruz long-toed (Ambystoma macrodactylum croceum)	8	3/11/1967	9/28/1977	RD(1)	7/2/1999	74	N/A	N/A	E	6C	Decreasing	3/5/2008	N/A
Salamander, Shenandoah (Plethodon shenandoah)	5	8/18/1989	9/29/1994	F	9/29/1994	21	N/A	N/A	E	8	Unknown	1/16/2008	N/A
Salamander, Sonora tiger (Ambystoma tigrinum stebbinsi)	2	1/6/1997	9/24/2002	F	9/24/2002	38	N/A	N/A	E	3	Unknown	4/21/2006	10/4/2007
Salamander, Texas blind (Typhlomolge rathbuni)	2	3/11/1967	4/8/1985	RF(1)	2/14/1996	36	N/A	N/A	E	5	Unknown	3/20/2008	N/A
Toad, arroyo (=arroyo southwestern) (Bufo californicus (=microscaphus))	8	12/16/1994	7/24/1999	F	7/24/1999	75	3,315,000	12	E	8	Decreasing	3/5/2008	N/A
Toad, Houston (Bufo houstonensis)	2	10/13/1970	9/17/1984	F	9/17/1984	23	N/A	N/A	E	2C	Decreasing	4/21/2006	N/A
Toad, Puerto Rican crested (Peltophryne lemur)	4	8/4/1987	8/7/1992	F	8/7/1992	17	N/A	N/A	T	2C	Improving	9/21/2007	N/A

*Earlier drafts and final plans for some individual species may have become incorporated into later multi-species or ecosystem plans.

www.fws.gov/endangered

1

Recovery Data as of September 30, 2008

GENERAL SPECIES INFORMATION					RECOVERY PLAN INFORMATION						SPECIES/RECOVERY STATUS		
Species Name	Lead Region	Date Listed	Date of First Final Plan	Plan Status*	Date of Current or Active Plan	Number of Actions Implemented	Estimated Costs for Recovery	Estimated Time to Recovery (years)	Listing Classification	Recovery Priority Number	FY 2008 Species' Status	Date 5-Year Status Review Initiated	Date 5-Year Status Review Completed
Toad, Wyoming (Bufo baxteri (=hemiophrys))	6	1/17/1984	9/11/1991	F	9/11/1991	34	N/A	N/A	E	2	Stable	N/A	N/A
Arachnids													
Harvestman, Bee Creek Cave (Texella reddelli)	2	9/16/1988	8/25/1994	F	8/25/1994	21	N/A	N/A	E	2C	Unknown	4/23/2007	N/A
Harvestman, Bone Cave (Texella reyesi)	2	9/16/1988	8/25/1994	F	8/25/1994	21	N/A	N/A	E	2C	Decreasing	4/23/2007	N/A
Harvestman, Cokendolpher Cave (Texella cokendolpheri)	2	12/26/2000	N/A	D	5/16/2008	25	140,628,000	25	E	2C	Decreasing	4/21/2006	N/A
Meshweaver, Braken Bat Cave (Cicurina venii)	2	12/26/2000	N/A	D	5/16/2008	25	140,628,000	25	E	2C	Decreasing	4/21/2006	N/A
Meshweaver, Government Canyon Bat Cave (Cicurina vespera)	2	12/26/2000	N/A	D	5/16/2008	25	140,628,000	25	E	2C	Decreasing	4/21/2006	N/A
Meshweaver, Madla's Cave (Cicurina madla)	2	12/26/2000	N/A	D	5/16/2008	25	140,628,000	25	E	2C	Decreasing	4/21/2006	N/A
Meshweaver, Robber Baron Cave (Cicurina baronia)	2	12/26/2000	N/A	D	5/16/2008	25	140,628,000	25	E	2C	Decreasing	4/21/2006	N/A
Pseudoscorpion, Tooth Cave (Tartarocreagris texana)	2	9/16/1988	8/25/1994	F	8/25/1994	21	N/A	N/A	E	2C	Unknown	4/23/2007	N/A
Spider, Government Canyon Bat Cave (Neoleptoneta microps)	2	12/26/2000	N/A	D	5/16/2008	25	140,628,000	25	E	2C	Decreasing	4/21/2006	N/A
Spider, Kauai cave wolf or pe'e pe'e maka 'ole (Adelocosa anops)	1	1/14/2000	7/19/2006	F	7/19/2006	18	3,445,000	30	E	1C	Stable	7/6/2005	9/29/2006
Spider, spruce-fir moss (Microhexura montivaga)	4	2/6/1995	9/11/1998	F	9/11/1998	10	N/A	N/A	E	5	Unknown	7/29/2008	N/A
Spider, Tooth Cave (Leptoneta myopica)	2	9/16/1988	8/25/1994	F	8/25/1994	21	N/A	N/A	E	2C	Unknown	4/23/2007	N/A
Birds													
'O'o, Kauai (honeyeater) (Moho braccatus)	1	3/11/1967	7/29/1983	RF(1)	9/22/2006	586	2,477,395,000	30	E	4	Unknown	7/6/2005	N/A
'O'u (honeycreeper) (Psittirostra psittacea)	1	3/11/1967	2/3/1983	RF(1)	9/22/2006	586	2,477,395,000	30	E	4	Unknown	7/6/2005	N/A
Akepa, Hawaii (honeycreeper) (Loxops coccineus coccineus)	1	10/13/1970	2/3/1983	RF(1)	9/22/2006	586	2,477,395,000	30	E	8	Stable	4/29/2008	N/A
Akepa, Maui (honeycreeper) (Loxops coccineus ochraceus)	1	10/13/1970	5/30/1984	RF(1)	9/22/2006	586	2,477,395,000	30	E	6	Unknown	4/11/2006	N/A
Akialoa, Kauai (honeycreeper) (Hemignathus procerus)	1	3/11/1967	7/29/1983	RF(1)	9/22/2006	586	2,477,395,000	30	E	5	Unknown	7/6/2005	N/A
Akiapola'au (honeycreeper) (Hemignathus munroi)	1	3/11/1967	2/3/1983	RF(1)	9/22/2006	586	2,477,395,000	30	E	2	Stable	4/29/2008	N/A
Albatross, short-tailed (Phoebastria (=Diomedea) albatrus)	7	6/2/1970	N/A	D	10/27/2005	55	5,673,000	25	E	8	Improving	N/A	N/A
Blackbird, yellow-shouldered (Agelaius xanthomus)	4	12/12/1976	5/25/1983	RF(1)	11/12/1996	19	N/A	N/A	E	2	Improving	9/21/2007	N/A
Bobwhite, masked (quail) (Colinus virginianus ridgwayi)	2	3/11/1967	1/1/1978	RF(2)	4/21/1995	56	N/A	N/A	E	6	Decreasing	N/A	N/A
Cahow (Pterodroma cahow)	10	6/2/1970	N/A	N/A	N/A	N/A	N/A	N/A	E	1	Unknown	9/21/2007	N/A

*Earlier drafts and final plans for some individual species may have become incorporated into later multi-species or ecosystem plans.

www.fws.gov/endangered

GENERAL SPECIES INFORMATION				RECOVERY PLAN INFORMATION						SPECIES/RECOVERY STATUS			
Species Name	Lead Region	Date Listed	Date of First Final Plan	Plan Status*	Date of Current or Active Plan	Number of Actions Implemented	Estimated Costs for Recovery	Estimated Time to Recovery (years)	Listing Classification	Recovery Priority Number	FY 2008 Species' Status	Date 5-Year Status Review Initiated	Date 5-Year Status Review Completed
Caracara, Audubon's crested (Polyborus plancus audubonii)	4	7/6/1987	5/18/1999	F	5/18/1999	1404	N/A	N/A	T	8C	Unknown	4/16/2008	N/A
Condor, California (Gymnogyps californianus)	8	3/11/1967	4/9/1975	RF(3)	4/25/1996	62	N/A	N/A	E	4C	Improving	N/A	N/A
Coot, Hawaiian (Fulica americana alai)	1	10/13/1970	6/19/1978	RD(2)	8/24/2005	57	N/A	N/A	E	8	Stable	4/29/2008	N/A
Crane, Mississippi sandhill (Grus canadensis pulla)	4	6/4/1973	9/14/1976	RF(3)	9/6/1991	17	N/A	N/A	E	6C	Stable	N/A	N/A
Crane, whooping (Grus americana)	2	3/11/1967	1/23/1980	RF(3)	5/29/2007	43	N/A	N/A	E	2C	Stable	N/A	N/A
Creeper, Hawaii (Oreomystis mana)	1	10/28/1975	2/3/1983	RF(1)	9/22/2006	586	2,477,395,000	30	E	8	Stable	4/29/2008	N/A
Creeper, Molokai (Paroreomyza flammea)	1	10/13/1970	5/30/1984	RF(1)	9/22/2006	586	2,477,395,000	30	E	5	Unknown	7/6/2005	N/A
Creeper, Oahu (Paroreomyza maculata)	1	10/13/1970	9/14/2006	RF(1)	9/22/2006	586	2,477,395,000	30	E	5	Unknown	4/11/2006	N/A
Crow, Hawaiian (='alala) (Corvus hawaiiensis)	1	3/11/1967	10/28/1982	RD(1)	12/18/2003	47	N/A	N/A	E	2C	Captivity	3/8/2007	N/A
Crow, Mariana (=aga) (Corvus kubaryi)	1	8/27/1984	9/28/1990	RD(1)	1/11/2006	61	N/A	N/A	E	5C	Decreasing	7/6/2005	N/A
Crow, white-necked (Corvus leucognaphalus)	4	4/3/1991	N/A	N/A	N/A	N/A	N/A	N/A	E	11	Presumed Extirpated	N/A	N/A
Curlew, Eskimo (Numenius borealis)	7	3/11/1967	N/A	E	N/A	N/A	N/A	N/A	E	5	Extinct	N/A	N/A
Duck, Hawaiian (=koloa) (Anas wyvilliana)	1	3/11/1967	6/19/1978	RD(2)	8/24/2005	57	N/A	N/A	E	2	Stable	3/8/2007	8/2/2007
Duck, Laysan (Anas laysanensis)	1	3/11/1967	12/17/1982	RD(1)	11/14/2004	27	N/A	N/A	E	2	Stable	7/6/2005	N/A
Eagle, bald (Sonoran desert DPS) (Haliaeetus leucocephalus)	2	5/1/2008	9/8/1982	F	9/8/1982	N/A	N/A	N/A	T	8	Stable	N/A	N/A
Eider, spectacled (Somateria fischeri)	7	5/10/1993	8/12/1996	F	8/12/1996	87	N/A	N/A	T	5	Unknown	N/A	N/A
Eider, Steller's (Polysticta stelleri)	7	6/11/1997	9/30/2002	F	9/30/2002	112	N/A	N/A	T	3	Unknown	N/A	N/A
Elepaio, Oahu (Chasiempis sandwichensis ibidis)	1	4/18/2000	9/14/2006	RF(1)	9/22/2006	586	2,477,395,000	30	E	3	Decreasing	3/8/2007	N/A
Falcon, northern aplomado (Falco femoralis septentrionalis)	2	2/25/1986	6/8/1990	F	6/8/1990	19	N/A	N/A	E	3	Improving	N/A	N/A
Finch, Laysan (honeycreeper) (Telespyza cantans)	1	3/11/1967	10/4/1984	F	10/4/1984	27	N/A	N/A	E	2	Decreasing	4/11/2006	1/18/2008
Finch, Nihoa (honeycreeper) (Telespyza ultima)	1	3/11/1967	10/4/1984	F	10/4/1984	27	N/A	N/A	E	2	Unknown	N/A	N/A
Flycatcher, southwestern willow (Empidonax traillii extimus)	2	2/27/1995	8/30/2002	F	8/30/2002	132	N/A	N/A	E	3C	Stable	3/20/2008	N/A
Gnatcatcher, coastal California (Polioptila californica californica)	8	3/30/1993	N/A	E	N/A	N/A	N/A	N/A	T	3C	Decreasing	3/5/2008	N/A
Goose, Hawaiian (Branta (=Nesochen) sandvicensis)	1	3/11/1967	2/14/1983	RD(1)	9/24/2004	58	N/A	N/A	E	2	Improving	N/A	N/A
Hawk, Hawaiian (='Io) (Buteo solitarius)	1	3/11/1967	5/9/1984	F	5/9/1984	12	N/A	N/A	E	14	Stable	3/8/2007	8/6/2008
Hawk, Puerto Rican broad-winged (Buteo platypterus brunnescens)	4	9/9/1994	9/8/1997	F	9/8/1997	16	N/A	N/A	E	6	Stable	9/21/2007	N/A

*Earlier drafts and final plans for some individual species may
have become incorporated into later multi-species or ecosystem plans.

www.fws.gov/endangered

GENERAL SPECIES INFORMATION			RECOVERY PLAN INFORMATION						SPECIES/RECOVERY STATUS				
Species Name	Lead Region	Date Listed	Date of First Final Plan	Plan Status*	Date of Current or Active Plan	Number of Actions Implemented	Estimated Costs for Recovery	Estimated Time to Recovery (years)	Listing Classification	Recovery Priority Number	FY 2008 Species' Status	Date 5-Year Status Review Initiated	Date 5-Year Status Review Completed
Hawk, Puerto Rican sharp-shinned (Accipiter striatus venator)	4	9/9/1994	9/8/1997	F	9/8/1997	16	N/A	N/A	E	3	Unknown	9/21/2007	N/A
Honeycreeper, crested (Palmeria dolei)	1	3/11/1967	5/30/1984	RF(1)	9/22/2006	586	2,477,395,000	30	E	7	Stable	N/A	N/A
Jay, Florida scrub (Aphelocoma coerulescens)	4	6/3/1987	5/9/1990	F	5/9/1990	19	N/A	N/A	T	8C	Decreasing	2/15/2006	9/28/2007
Kingfisher, Guam Micronesian (Halcyon cinnamomina cinnamomina)	1	8/27/1984	9/28/1990	RF(1)	11/14/2008	N/A	145,830,000	50	E	6	Cap ivity	4/11/2006	1/18/2008
Kite, Everglade snail (Rostrhamus sociabilis plumbeus)	4	3/11/1967	3/11/1983	F	5/18/1999	1404	N/A	N/A	E	3C	Decreasing	9/27/2006	9/30/2007
Megapode, Micronesian (Megapodius laperouse)	1	6/2/1970	4/10/1998	F	4/10/1998	16	3,677,000	15	E	9	Stable	4/29/2008	N/A
Millerbird, Nihoa (old world warbler) (Acrocephalus familiaris kingi)	1	3/11/1967	10/4/1984	F	10/4/1984	27	N/A	N/A	E	2	Unknown	4/29/2008	N/A
Moorhen, Hawaiian common (Gallinula chloropus sandvicensis)	1	3/11/1967	6/19/1978	RD(2)	8/24/2005	57	N/A	N/A	E	9	Stable	4/29/2008	N/A
Moorhen, Mariana common (Gallinula chloropus guam)	1	8/27/1984	9/30/1991	F	9/30/1991	73	N/A	N/A	E	9C	Stable	3/8/2007	N/A
Murrelet, marbled (Brachyramphus marmoratus)	1	10/1/1992	9/24/1997	F	9/24/1997	35	N/A	N/A	T	2C	Decreasing	4/21/2003	9/1/2004
Nightjar, Puerto Rican (Caprimulgus noctitherus)	4	6/4/1973	4/19/1984	F	4/19/1984	7	N/A	N/A	E	5C	Stable	N/A	N/A
Nukupu'u (honeycreeper) (Hemignathus lucidus)	1	3/11/1967	7/29/1983	RF(1)	9/22/2006	586	2,477,395,000	30	E	5	Unknown	4/11/2006	N/A
Owl, Mexican spotted (Strix occidentalis lucida)	2	3/16/1993	10/16/1995	F	10/16/1995	157	N/A	N/A	T	9C	Stable	N/A	N/A
Owl, northern spotted (Strix occidentalis caurina)	1	6/26/1990	5/13/2008	F	5/13/2008	34	489,200,000	30	T	3C	Decreasing	4/21/2003	11/15/2004
Palila (honeycreeper) (Loxioides bailleui)	1	3/11/1967	1/23/1978	RF(1)	9/22/2006	586	2,477,395,000	30	E	1	Decreasing	3/8/2007	N/A
Parrot, Puerto Rican (Amazona vittata)	4	3/11/1967	11/30/1982	F	6/17/2008	29	14,723,000	13	E	2	Stable	9/12/2005	9/26/2008
Parrotbill, Maui (honeycreeper) (Pseudonestor xanthophrys)	1	3/11/1967	5/30/1984	RF(1)	9/22/2006	586	2,477,395,000	30	E	1	Stable	N/A	N/A
Pelican, brown (Pelecanus occidentalis)	8	6/2/1970	12/24/1986	F	02/03/1983, 12/24/1986	63	N/A	N/A	E	9	Stable	5/24/2006	2/7/2007
Petrel, Hawaiian dark-rumped (Pterodroma phaeopygia sandwichensis)	1	3/11/1967	4/25/1983	F	4/25/1983	38	N/A	N/A	E	2	Unknown	N/A	N/A
Pigeon, Puerto Rican plain (Columba inornata wetmorei)	4	10/13/1970	10/14/1982	F	10/14/1982	40	N/A	N/A	E	3C	Stable	9/12/2005	N/A
Plover, piping (Great Lakes watershed) (Charadrius melodus)	3	12/11/1985	9/16/2003	F	9/16/2003	53	N/A	N/A	E	2C	Stable	N/A	N/A
Plover, piping (except Great Lakes watershed) (Charadrius melodus)	5	12/11/1985	3/31/1988	RF(1), F	05/02/1996, 05/12/1988	40	N/A	N/A	T	2C	Stable	9/30/2008	N/A

*Earlier drafts and final plans for some individual species may have become incorporated into later multi-species or ecosystem plans.

www.fws.gov/endangered

Species Name	Lead Region	Date Listed	Date of First Final Plan	Plan Status*	Date of Current or Active Plan	Number of Actions Implemented	Estimated Costs for Recovery	Estimated Time to Recovery (years)	Listing Classification	Recovery Priority Number	FY 2008 Species' Status	Date 5-Year Status Review Initiated	Date 5-Year Status Review Completed
Plover, western snowy (Charadrius alexandrinus nivosus)	8	3/5/1993	N/A	F	9/24/2007	94	149,946,000	40	T	3C	Decreasing	3/22/2004	6/8/2006
Po'ouli (honeycreeper) (Melamprosops phaeosoma)	1	10/28/1975	5/30/1984	RF(1)	9/22/2006	586	2,477,395,000	30	E	4	Unknown	4/11/2006	N/A
Prairie-chicken, Attwater's greater (Tympanuchus cupido attwateri)	2	3/11/1967	12/16/1983	RD(2)	11/19/2007	58	124,086,000	50	E	3	Stable	4/23/2007	N/A
Rail, California clapper (Rallus longirostris obsoletus)	8	10/13/1970	11/16/1984	F	11/16/1984	69	N/A	N/A	E	3C	Stable	N/A	N/A
Rail, Guam (Rallus owstoni)	1	4/11/1984	9/28/1990	F	9/28/1990	86	N/A	N/A	E	2	Captivity	3/8/2007	N/A
Rail, light-footed clapper (Rallus longirostris levipes)	8	10/13/1970	7/3/1979	RF(1)	6/24/1985	216	N/A	N/A	E	6	Decreasing	3/5/2008	N/A
Rail, Yuma clapper (Rallus longirostris yumanensis)	2	3/11/1967	2/4/1983	F	2/4/1983	34	N/A	N/A	E	6	Stable	2/2/2005	9/11/2006
Shearwater, Newell's Townsend's (Puffinus auricularis newelli)	1	10/28/1975	4/25/1983	F	4/25/1983	38	N/A	N/A	T	3	Decreasing	4/29/2008	N/A
Shrike, San Clemente loggerhead (Lanius ludovicianus mearnsi)	8	9/12/1977	1/26/1984	F	1/26/1984	54	N/A	N/A	E	12	Stable	2/14/2007	N/A
Sparrow, Cape Sable seaside (Ammodramus maritimus mirabilis)	4	3/11/1967	5/18/1999	F	5/18/1999	1404	N/A	N/A	E	3C	Decreasing	6/21/2005	N/A
Sparrow, Florida grasshopper (Ammodramus savannarum floridanus)	4	7/31/1986	5/18/1999	F	5/18/1999	1404	N/A	N/A	E	3C	Decreasing	4/26/2007	9/30/2008
Sparrow, San Clemente sage (Amphispiza belli clementeae)	8	9/12/1977	1/26/1984	F	1/26/1984	54	N/A	N/A	T	9	Stable	3/5/2008	N/A
Stilt, Hawaiian (Himantopus mexicanus knudseni)	1	10/13/1970	6/19/1978	RD(2)	8/24/2005	57	N/A	N/A	E	9	Stable	4/29/2008	N/A
Stork, wood (Mycteria americana)	4	2/28/1984	9/9/1986	RF(1)	1/27/1997	35	N/A	N/A	E	5C	Stable	9/27/2006	9/21/2007
Swiftlet, Mariana gray (Aerodramus vanikorensis bartschi)	1	8/27/1984	9/30/1991	F	9/30/1991	40	N/A	N/A	E	8	Stable	4/29/2008	N/A
Tern, California least (Sterna antillarum browni)	8	6/2/1970	4/2/1980	RF(1)	9/27/1985	101	N/A	N/A	E	18C	Decreasing	7/7/2005	9/26/2006
Tern, least (Sterna antillarum)	3	5/28/1985	9/19/1990	F	9/19/1990	82	2,000,000	15	E	3C	Unknown	4/22/2008	N/A
Tern, roseate (Western hemisphere, except NE U.S.) (Sterna dougallii dougallii)	4	11/2/1987	9/24/1993	F	9/24/1993	18	N/A	N/A	T	3	Improving	N/A	N/A
Tern, roseate (northeast U.S. nesting population) (Sterna dougallii dougallii)	5	11/2/1987	3/20/1989	RF(1)	11/5/1998	32	N/A	N/A	E	3	Decreasing	N/A	N/A
Thrush, large Kauai (=kamao) (Myadestes myadestinus)	1	10/13/1970	7/29/1983	RF(1)	9/22/2006	586	2,477,395,000	30	E	5	Unknown	7/6/2005	N/A
Thrush, Molokai (Myadestes lanaiensis rutha)	1	10/13/1970	5/30/1984	RF(1)	9/22/2006	586	2,477,395,000	30	E	5	Unknown	7/6/2005	N/A
Thrush, small Kauai (=puaiohi) (Myadestes palmeri)	1	3/11/1967	7/29/1983	RF(1)	9/22/2006	586	2,477,395,000	30	E	2	Stable	3/8/2007	N/A
Towhee, Inyo California (Pipilo crissalis eremophilus)	8	8/3/1987	4/10/1998	F	4/10/1998	19	N/A	N/A	T	15	Improving	3/22/2006	9/30/2008

*Earlier drafts and final plans for some individual species may have become incorporated into later multi-species or ecosystem plans.

www.fws.gov/endangered

GENERAL SPECIES INFORMATION			RECOVERY PLAN INFORMATION							SPECIES/RECOVERY STATUS			
Species Name	Lead Region	Date Listed	Date of First Final Plan	Plan Status*	Date of Current or Active Plan	Number of Actions Implemented	Estimated Costs for Recovery	Estimated Time to Recovery (years)	Listing Classification	Recovery Priority Number	FY 2008 Species' Status	Date 5-Year Status Review Initiated	Date 5-Year Status Review Completed
Vireo, black-capped (Vireo atricapilla)	2	10/6/1987	9/30/1991	F	9/30/1991	31	N/A	N/A	E	8	Stable	2/2/2005	7/26/2007
Vireo, least Bell's (Vireo belli pusillus)	8	5/2/1986	N/A	D	5/6/1998	49	N/A	N/A	E	9	Stable	7/7/2005	9/26/2006
Warbler (=wood), Bachman's (Vermivora bachmanii)	4	3/11/1967	N/A	E	N/A	N/A	N/A	N/A	E	5	Presumed Extinct	7/26/2005	2/9/2007
Warbler (=wood), golden-cheeked (Dendroica chrysoparia)	2	5/4/1990	9/30/1992	F	9/30/1992	45	11,889,000	16	E	2C	Decreasing	4/21/2006	N/A
Warbler (=wood), Kirtland's (Dendroica kirtlandii)	3	3/11/1967	8/11/1978	F	8/11/1978	37	N/A	N/A	E	2C	Improving	7/27/2007	N/A
Warbler, nightingale reed (old world warbler) (Acrocephalus luscinia)	1	6/2/1970	4/10/1998	F	4/10/1998	17	4,150,000	15	E	8C	Decreasing	3/8/2007	N/A
White-eye, bridled (Zosterops conspicillatus conspicillatus)	1	8/27/1984	9/28/1990	F	9/28/1990	86	N/A	N/A	E	6	Presumed Extinct	3/8/2007	N/A
White-eye, Rota bridled (Zosterops rotensis)	1	1/22/2004	10/19/2007	F	10/19/2007	36	N/A	N/A	E	2	Stable	4/29/2008	N/A
Woodpecker, ivory-billed (Campephilus principalis)	4	3/11/1967	N/A	D	8/22/2007	N/A	N/A	N/A	E	5	Unknown	N/A	N/A
Woodpecker, red-cockaded (Picoides borealis)	4	10/13/1970	8/24/1979	RF(2)	3/20/2003	264	N/A	N/A	E	8C	Improving	9/12/2005	10/5/2006
Clams													
Acornshell, southern (Epioblasma othcaloogensis)	4	3/17/1993	11/17/2000	F	11/17/2000	29	N/A	N/A	E	5	Presumed Extinct	6/14/2005	4/7/2008
Bankclimber, purple (mussel) (Elliptoideus sloatianus)	4	3/16/1998	9/30/2003	F	9/30/2003	28	N/A	N/A	T	11	Decreasing	9/27/2006	9/17/2007
Bean, Cumberland (pearlymussel) (Villosa trabalis)	4	6/14/1976	8/22/1984	F	8/22/1984	18	N/A	N/A	E	5C	Stable	7/26/2005	N/A
Bean, purple (Villosa perpurpurea)	5	1/10/1997	5/24/2004	F	5/24/2004	26	N/A	N/A	E	5	Decreasing	4/21/2006	10/24/2006
Blossom, green (pearlymussel) (Epioblasma torulosa gubernaculum)	4	6/14/1976	7/9/1984	F	7/9/1984	18	N/A	N/A	E	6	Presumed Extinct	9/20/2005	9/21/2007
Blossom, tubercled (pearlymussel) (Epioblasma torulosa torulosa)	4	6/14/1976	1/25/1985	F	1/25/1985	4	N/A	N/A	E	6	Presumed Extinct	9/20/2005	N/A
Blossom, turgid (pearlymussel) (Epioblasma turgidula)	4	6/14/1976	1/25/1985	F	1/25/1985	4	N/A	N/A	E	5	Presumed Extinct	9/20/2005	9/21/2007
Blossom, yellow (pearlymussel) (Epioblasma florentina florentina)	4	6/14/1976	1/25/1985	F	1/25/1985	4	N/A	N/A	E	6	Presumed Extinct	9/20/2005	9/21/2007
Catspaw (=purple cat's paw pearlymussel) (Epioblasma obliquata obliquata)	3	7/10/1990	3/10/1992	F	3/10/1992	13	N/A	N/A	E	6	Decreasing	N/A	N/A
Catspaw, white (pearlymussel) (Epioblasma obliquata perobliqua)	3	6/14/1976	1/25/1990	F	1/25/1990	16	N/A	N/A	E	6C	Decreasing	7/27/2007	N/A
Clubshell (Pleurobema clava)	5	1/22/1993	9/21/1994	F	9/21/1994	25	2,722,000	25	E	5	Decreasing Presumed	4/21/2006	N/A
Clubshell, black (Pleurobema curtum)	4	4/7/1987	11/14/1989	F	11/14/1989	7	N/A	N/A	E	5C	Extinct	9/8/2006	N/A
Clubshell, ovate (Pleurobema perovatum)	4	3/17/1993	11/17/2000	F	11/17/2000	29	N/A	N/A	E	5	Unknown	6/14/2005	4/7/2008
Clubshell, southern (Pleurobema decisum)	4	3/17/1993	11/17/2000	F	11/17/2000	29	N/A	N/A	E	8	Unknown	6/14/2005	4/7/2008

*Earlier drafts and final plans for some individual species may have become incorporated into later multi-species or ecosystem plans.

www.fws.gov/endangered

Species Name	GENERAL SPECIES INFORMATION Lead Region	Date Listed	Date of First Final Plan	RECOVERY PLAN INFORMATION Plan Status*	Date of Current or Active Plan	Number of Actions Implemented	Estimated Costs for Recovery	Estimated Time to Recovery (years)	SPECIES/RECOVERY STATUS Listing Classification	Recovery Priority Number	FY 2008 Species' Status	Date 5-Year Status Review Initiated	Date 5-Year Status Review Completed
Combshell, Cumberlandian (Epioblasma brevidens)	4	1/10/1997	5/24/2004	F	5/24/2004	26	N/A	N/A	E	5	Stable	9/20/2005	9/19/2007
Combshell, southern (Epioblasma penita)	4	4/7/1987	11/14/1989	F	11/14/1989	7	N/A	N/A	E	2C	Unknown	9/8/2006	N/A
Combshell, upland (Epioblasma metastriata)	4	3/17/1993	11/17/2000	F	11/17/2000	29	N/A	N/A	E	5	Presumed Extinct	6/14/2005	4/7/2008
Elktoe, Appalachian (Alasmidonta raveneliana)	4	11/23/1994	8/26/1996	F	8/26/1996	13	422,500	N/A	E	5C	Decreasing	9/20/2005	N/A
Elktoe, Cumberland (Alasmidonta atropurpurea)	4	1/10/1997	5/24/2004	F	5/24/2004	26	N/A	N/A	E	5	Stable	9/20/2005	1/24/2007
Fanshell (Cyprogenia stegania)	4	6/21/1990	7/9/1991	F	7/9/1991	12	N/A	N/A	E	5	Stable	7/29/2008	N/A
Fatmucket, Arkansas (Lampsilis powellii)	4	4/5/1990	2/10/1992	F	2/10/1992	12	N/A	N/A	T	8	Decreasing	9/8/2006	N/A
Heelsplitter, Alabama (=inflated) (Potamilus inflatus)	4	9/28/1990	4/13/1993	F	4/13/1993	8	N/A	N/A	T	8C	Unknown	7/29/2008	N/A
Heelsplitter, Carolina (Lasmigona decorata)	4	6/30/1993	1/17/1997	F	1/17/1997	14	422,500	N/A	E	5C	Decreasing	7/28/2006	N/A
Higgins eye (pearlymussel) (Lampsilis higginsii)	3	6/14/1976	7/29/1983	RF(1)	7/14/2004	50	N/A	N/A	E	5C	Decreasing	7/19/2005	5/9/2006
Kidneyshell, triangular (Ptychobranchus greenii)	4	3/17/1993	11/17/2000	F	11/17/2000	29	N/A	N/A	E	8	Unknown	6/14/2005	4/7/2008
Lampmussel, Alabama (Lampsilis virescens)	4	6/14/1976	7/2/1985	F	7/2/1985	17	N/A	N/A	E	5	Unknown	N/A	N/A
Lilliput, pale (pearlymussel) (Toxolasma cylindrellus)	4	6/14/1976	8/22/1984	F	8/22/1984	18	N/A	N/A	E	5	Unknown	N/A	N/A
Mapleleaf, winged (Quadrula fragosa)	3	6/20/1991	6/25/1997	F	6/25/1997	77	N/A	N/A	E	2C	Stable	N/A	N/A
Moccasinshell, Alabama (Medionidus acutissimus)	4	3/17/1993	11/17/2000	F	11/17/2000	29	N/A	N/A	T	8	Unknown	6/14/2005	4/7/2008
Moccasinshell, Coosa (Medionidus parvulus)	4	3/17/1993	11/17/2000	F	11/17/2000	29	N/A	N/A	E	5	Unknown	6/14/2005	4/7/2008
Moccasinshell, Gulf (Medionidus penicillatus)	4	3/16/1998	9/30/2003	F	9/30/2003	28	N/A	N/A	E	5	Unknown	9/27/2006	9/17/2007
Moccasinshell, Ochlockonee (Medionidus simpsonianus)	4	3/16/1998	9/30/2003	F	9/30/2003	28	N/A	N/A	E	5	Unknown	9/27/2006	9/17/2007
Monkeyface, Appalachian (pearlymussel) (Quadrula sparsa)	5	6/14/1976	7/9/1984	F	7/9/1984	25	N/A	N/A	E	5	Decreasing	N/A	N/A
Monkeyface, Cumberland (pearlymussel) (Quadrula intermedia)	4	6/14/1976	7/9/1984	F	7/9/1984	18	N/A	N/A	E	5C	Decreasing	9/20/2005	N/A
Mucket, orangenacre (Lampsilis perovalis)	4	3/17/1993	11/17/2000	F	11/17/2000	29	N/A	N/A	T	8	Unknown	6/14/2005	4/7/2008
Mucket, pink (pearlymussel) (Lampsilis abrupta)	4	6/14/1976	1/24/1985	F	1/24/1985	6	N/A	N/A	E	5	Stable	7/29/2008	N/A
Mussel, oyster (Epioblasma capsaeformis)	4	1/10/1997	5/24/2004	F	5/24/2004	26	N/A	N/A	E	5	Stable	9/20/2005	N/A
Mussel, scaleshell (Leptodea leptodon)	3	10/9/2001	N/A	D	8/6/2004	45	38,613,000	50	E	2	Decreasing	10/4/2007	N/A

*Earlier drafts and final plans for some individual species may have become incorporated into later multi-species or ecosystem plans.

www.fws.gov/endangered

Recovery Data as of September 30, 2008

GENERAL SPECIES INFORMATION			RECOVERY PLAN INFORMATION						SPECIES/RECOVERY STATUS				
Species Name	Lead Region	Date Listed	Date of First Final Plan	Plan Status*	Date of Current or Active Plan	Number of Actions Implemented	Estimated Costs for Recovery	Estimated Time to Recovery (years)	Listing Classifi-cation	Recovery Priority Number	FY 2008 Species' Status	Date 5-Year Status Review Initiated	Date 5-Year Status Review Completed
Pearlshell, Louisiana (Margaritifera hembeli)	4	2/5/1988	12/3/1990	F	12/3/1990	6	N/A	N/A	T	8	Unknown	9/8/2006	N/A
Pearlymussel, birdwing (Conradilla caelata)	4	6/14/1976	7/9/1984	F	7/9/1984	18	N/A	N/A	E	4C	Stable	7/28/2006	N/A
Pearlymussel, cracking (Hemistena lata)	4	9/28/1989	7/11/1991	F	7/11/1991	12	N/A	N/A	E	4	Unknown	7/28/2006	N/A
Pearlymussel, Cur is (Epioblasma florentina curtisii)	3	6/14/1976	2/4/1986	F	2/4/1986	19	N/A	N/A	E	6	Decreasing	9/21/2006	N/A
Pearlymussel, dromedary (Dromus dromas)	4	6/14/1976	7/9/1984	F	7/9/1984	18	N/A	N/A	E	4C	Stable	7/28/2006	N/A
Pearlymussel, littlewing (Pegias fabula)	4	11/14/1988	9/22/1989	F	9/22/1989	10	N/A	N/A	E	4	Decreasing	7/28/2006	N/A
Pigtoe, Cumberland (Pleurobema gibberum)	4	5/7/1991	8/13/1992	F	8/13/1992	14	618,500	N/A	E	5	Unknown	9/21/2007	N/A
Pigtoe, dark (Pleurobema furvum)	4	3/17/1993	11/17/2000	F	11/17/2000	29	N/A	N/A	E	5	Unknown	6/14/2005	4/7/2008
Pigtoe, finerayed (Fusconaia cuneolus)	4	6/14/1976	9/19/1984	F	9/19/1984	15	N/A	N/A	E	5	Decreasing	7/28/2006	N/A
Pigtoe, flat (Pleurobema marshalli)	4	4/7/1987	11/14/1989	F	11/14/1989	7	N/A	N/A	E	5	Extinct	9/8/2006	N/A
Pigtoe, heavy (Pleurobema taitianum)	4	4/7/1987	11/14/1989	F	11/14/1989	7	N/A	N/A	E	5C	Unknown	9/8/2006	N/A
Pigtoe, oval (Pleurobema pyriforme)	4	3/16/1998	9/30/2003	F	9/30/2003	28	N/A	N/A	E	5	Unknown	9/27/2006	9/17/2007
Pigtoe, rough (Pleurobema plenum)	4	6/14/1976	8/6/1984	F	8/6/1984	18	N/A	N/A	E	5	Stable	9/21/2007	N/A
Pigtoe, shiny (Fusconaia cor)	4	6/14/1976	7/9/1984	F	7/9/1984	12	N/A	N/A	E	5	Stable	7/28/2006	N/A
Pigtoe, sou hern (Pleurobema georgianum)	4	3/17/1993	11/17/2000	F	11/17/2000	29	N/A	N/A	E	5	Unknown	6/14/2005	4/7/2008
Pimpleback, orangefoot (pearlymussel) (Plethobasus cooperianus)	4	6/14/1976	9/30/1984	F	9/30/1984	18	N/A	N/A	E	5	Stable	9/21/2007	N/A
Pocketbook, fat (Potamilus capax)	4	6/14/1976	10/4/1985	F	11/14/1989	10	N/A	N/A	E	8	Unknown	8/2/2007	N/A
Pocketbook, finelined (Lampsilis altilis)	4	3/17/1993	11/17/2000	F	11/17/2000	29	N/A	N/A	T	8	Unknown	6/14/2005	4/7/2008
Pocketbook, Ouachita rock (Arkansia wheeleri)	2	10/23/1991	9/27/2002	F	6/2/2004	43	N/A	N/A	E	4C	Decreasing	4/23/2007	N/A
Pocketbook, shinyrayed (Lampsilis subangulata)	4	3/16/1998	9/30/2003	F	9/30/2003	28	N/A	N/A	E	5	Unknown	9/27/2006	9/17/2007
Pocketbook, speckled (Lampsilis streckeri)	4	2/28/1989	1/2/1992	F	1/2/1992	12	N/A	N/A	E	8	Stable	7/26/2005	1/9/2007
Rabbitsfoot, rough (Quadrula cylindrica strigillata)	5	1/10/1997	5/24/2004	F	5/24/2004	26	N/A	N/A	E	6	Decreasing	1/16/2008	N/A
Riffleshell, northern (Epioblasma torulosa rangiana)	5	1/22/1993	9/21/1994	F	9/21/1994	25	2,772,000	25	E	6	Stable	4/21/2006	N/A
Riffleshell, tan (Epioblasma florentina walkeri (=E. walkeri)	4	9/26/1977	10/22/1984	F	10/22/1984	12	N/A	N/A	E	5	Decreasing	9/21/2007	N/A
Ring pink (mussel) (Obovaria retusa)	4	9/29/1989	3/25/1991	F	3/25/1991	12	N/A	N/A	E	5	Decreasing	7/28/2006	N/A
Slabshell, Chipola (Elliptio chipolaensis)	4	3/16/1998	9/30/2003	F	9/30/2003	28	N/A	N/A	T	11	Stable	9/27/2006	9/17/2007
Spinymussel, James (Pleurobema collina) (Elliptio collina)	5	7/22/1988	9/24/1990	F	9/24/1990	14	N/A	N/A	E	8	Stable	1/16/2008	N/A
Spinymussel, Tar River (Elliptio steinstansana)	4	6/27/1985	1/16/1987	RF(1)	5/5/1992	14	N/A	N/A	E	5C	Decreasing	N/A	N/A

*Earlier drafts and final plans for some individual species may have become incorporated into later multi-species or ecosystem plans.

www.fws.gov/endangered

GENERAL SPECIES INFORMATION					RECOVERY PLAN INFORMATION				SPECIES/RECOVERY STATUS				
Species Name	Lead Region	Date Listed	Date of First Final Plan	Plan Status*	Date of Current or Active Plan	Number of Actions Implemented	Estimated Costs for Recovery	Estimated Time to Recovery (years)	Listing Classification	Recovery Priority Number	FY 2008 Species' Status	Date 5-Year Status Review Initiated	Date 5-Year Status Review Completed
Stirrupshell (Quadrula stapes)	4	4/7/1987	11/14/1989	F	11/14/1989	7	N/A	N/A	E	5	Extinct	9/8/2006	N/A
Three-ridge, fat (mussel) (Amblema neisleni)	4	3/16/1998	9/30/2003	F	9/30/2003	28	N/A	N/A	E	5	Decreasing	9/27/2006	9/17/2007
Wartyback, white (pearlymussel) (Plethobasus cicatricosus)	4	6/14/1976	9/19/1984	F	9/19/1984	18	N/A	N/A	E	5	Unknown	9/21/2007	N/A
Wedgemussel, dwarf (Alasmidonta heterodon)	5	3/14/1990	2/8/1993	F	2/8/1993	17	N/A	N/A	E	5	Unknown	4/21/2006	7/25/2007
Conifers and Cycads													
Cypress, Gowen (Cupressus goveniana ssp. goveniana)	8	8/12/1998	12/20/2004	F	6/17/2005	46	N/A	N/A	T	8C	Stable	2/14/2007	3/31/2008
Cypress, Santa Cruz (Cupressus abramsiana)	8	1/8/1987	9/26/1998	F	9/26/1998	26	51,500	5	E	14	Stable	2/14/2007	N/A
Torreya, Florida (Torreya taxifolia)	4	1/23/1984	9/9/1986	F	9/9/1986	40	N/A	N/A	E	5	Unknown	N/A	N/A
Crustaceans													
Amphipod, Hay's Spring (Stygobromus hayi)	5	2/5/1982	N/A	E	N/A	N/A	N/A	N/A	E	5	Stable	1/29/2007	12/19/2007
Amphipod, Illinois cave (Gammarus acherondytes)	3	9/3/1998	9/20/2002	F	9/20/2002	28	8,250,000	20	E	2C	Unknown	4/22/2008	N/A
Amphipod, Kauai cave (Spelaeorchestia koloana)	1	1/14/2000	7/19/2006	F	7/19/2006	18	3,445,000	30	E	1C	Stable	7/6/2005	9/29/2006
Amphipod, Noel's (Gammarus desperatus)	2	8/9/2005	N/A	N/A	N/A	N/A	N/A	N/A	E	5	Stable	N/A	N/A
Amphipod, Peck's cave (Stygobromus (=Stygonectes) pecki)	2	12/18/1997	N/A	N/A	N/A	N/A	N/A	N/A	E	2C	Stable	3/20/2008	N/A
Crayfish, cave (Cambarus aculabrum)	4	4/27/1993	10/30/1996	F	10/30/1996	11	N/A	N/A	E	5	Stable	7/29/2008	N/A
Crayfish, cave (Cambarus zophonastes)	4	4/7/1987	9/26/1988	F	9/26/1988	10	N/A	N/A	E	5	Stable	8/2/2007	N/A
Crayfish, Nashville (Orconectes shoupi)	4	9/26/1986	8/12/1987	RF(1)	2/8/1989	11	N/A	N/A	E	11C	Stable	9/21/2007	N/A
Crayfish, Shasta (Pacifastacus fortis)	8	9/30/1988	8/28/1998	F	8/28/1998	81	4,500,000	15	E	5	Decreasing	3/5/2008	N/A
Fairy shrimp, Conservancy (Branchinecta conservatio)	8	9/19/1994	3/7/2006	F	12/15/2005	192	N/A	N/A	E	8	Stable	3/22/2006	9/24/2007
Fairy shrimp, longhorn (Branchinecta longiantenna)	8	9/19/1994	3/7/2006	F	12/15/2005	192	N/A	N/A	E	8	Unknown	3/22/2006	9/28/2007
Fairy shrimp, Riverside (Streptocephalus wootoni)	8	8/3/1993	9/3/1998	F	9/3/1998	14	N/A	N/A	E	5C	Decreasing	3/22/2006	9/30/2008
Fairy shrimp, San Diego (Branchinecta sandiegonensis)	8	2/3/1997	9/3/1998	F	9/3/1998	14	N/A	N/A	E	2C	Stable	3/22/2006	9/30/2008
Fairy shrimp, vernal pool (Branchinecta lynchi)	8	9/19/1994	3/7/2006	F	12/15/2005	192	N/A	N/A	T	2C	Unknown	3/22/2006	9/28/2007
Isopod, Lee County cave (Lirceus usdagalun)	5	11/20/1992	9/30/1997	F	9/30/1997	21	N/A	N/A	E	8	Unknown	1/29/2007	9/30/2008
Isopod, Madison Cave (Antrolana lira)	5	10/4/1982	9/30/1996	F	9/30/1996	10	419,000	10	T	4	Unknown	N/A	N/A
Isopod, Socorro (Thermosphaeroma thermophilus)	2	4/26/1978	2/16/1982	F	2/16/1982	17	N/A	N/A	E	2	Stable	3/20/2008	N/A

*Earlier drafts and final plans for some individual species may have become incorporated into later multi-species or ecosystem plans.

www.fws.gov/endangered

GENERAL SPECIES INFORMATION			RECOVERY PLAN INFORMATION						SPECIES/RECOVERY STATUS				
Species Name	Lead Region	Date Listed	Date of First Final Plan	Plan Status*	Date of Current or Active Plan	Number of Actions Implemented	Estimated Costs for Recovery	Estimated Time to Recovery (years)	Listing Classification	Recovery Priority Number	FY 2008 Species' Status	Date 5-Year Status Review Initiated	Date 5-Year Status Review Completed
Shrimp, Alabama cave (Palaemonias alabamae)	4	9/7/1988	9/4/1997	F	9/4/1997	14	N/A	N/A	E	5	Stable	6/14/2005	8/29/2006
Shrimp, California freshwater (Syncaris pacifica)	8	10/31/1988	7/31/1998	F	7/31/1998	42	39,747,000	10	E	8C	Unknown	3/22/2006	1/10/2008
Shrimp, Kentucky cave (Palaemonias ganteri)	4	10/12/1983	10/7/1988	F	10/7/1988	11	N/A	N/A	E	5	Unknown	9/21/2007	N/A
Shrimp, Squirrel Chimney Cave (Palaemonetes cummingi)	4	6/21/1990	N/A	E	N/A	N/A	N/A	N/A	T	5C	Unknown	4/26/2007	6/28/2008
Tadpole shrimp, vernal pool (Lepidurus packardi)	8	9/19/1994	3/7/2006	F	12/15/2005	192	N/A	N/A	E	2C	Unknown	2/22/2006	9/28/2007
Ferns and Allies													
Diellia, asplenium-leaved (Diellia erecta)	1	11/10/1994	7/10/1999	F	7/10/1999	56	33,500,000	11	E	2	Decreasing	3/8/2007	N/A
Fern, Alabama streak-sorus (Thelypteris pilosa var. alabamensis)	4	7/8/1992	10/25/1996	F	10/25/1996	8	N/A	N/A	T	9	Stable	9/8/2006	N/A
Fern, Aleutian shield (Polystichum aleuticum)	7	2/17/1988	9/30/1992	F	9/30/1992	N/A	N/A	N/A	E	8	Stable	8/31/2005	9/26/2007
Fern, American hart's-tongue (Asplenium scolopendrium var. americanum)	4	7/14/1989	9/15/1993	F	9/15/1993	16	373,200	6	T	9	Unknown	7/28/2006	N/A
Fern, Elfin tree (Cyathea dryopteroides)	4	6/16/1987	1/31/1991	F	1/31/1991	19	N/A	N/A	E	5	Unknown	9/27/2006	N/A
Fern, pendant kihi (Adenophorus periens)	1	11/10/1994	7/10/1999	F	7/10/1999	56	33,900,000	11	E	11	Decreasing	4/29/2008	N/A
Ihi'ihi (Marsilea villosa)	1	6/22/1992	4/18/1996	F	4/18/1996	65	N/A	N/A	E	8	Improving	N/A	N/A
No common name (Adiantum vivesii)	4	6/9/1993	1/17/1995	F	1/17/1995	19	N/A	N/A	E	17	Stable	9/12/2005	6/10/2008
No common name (Asplenium fragile var. insulare)	1	9/26/1994	4/10/1998	F	4/10/1998	23	4,742,000	15	E	6	Decreasing	N/A	N/A
No common name (Diellia falcata)	1	10/29/1991	8/10/1998	F	8/10/1998	28	N/A	N/A	E	8	Decreasing	N/A	N/A
No common name (Diellia pallida)	1	2/25/1994	9/20/1995	F	9/20/1995	89	N/A	N/A	E	5	Decreasing	4/11/2006	1/18/2008
No common name (Diellia unisora)	1	6/27/1994	8/10/1998	F	8/10/1998	28	N/A	N/A	E	11	Decreasing	N/A	N/A
No common name (Diplazium molokaiense)	1	9/26/1994	4/10/1998	F	4/10/1998	23	4,742,000	15	E	5	Decreasing	4/29/2008	N/A
No common name (Elaphoglossum serpens)	4	6/9/1993	1/17/1995	F	1/17/1995	19	N/A	N/A	E	5	Unknown	9/27/2006	N/A
No common name (Polystichum calderonense)	4	6/9/1993	1/17/1995	F	1/17/1995	19	N/A	N/A	E	5	Unknown	9/27/2006	N/A
No common name (Pteris lidgatei)	1	9/26/1994	4/10/1998	F	4/10/1998	23	4,742,000	15	E	5	Decreasing	3/8/2007	N/A
No common name (Tectaria estremerana)	4	6/9/1993	1/17/1995	F	1/17/1995	19	N/A	N/A	E	8	Unknown	9/27/2006	N/A
No common name (Thelypteris inabonensis)	4	7/2/1993	1/17/1995	F	1/17/1995	19	N/A	N/A	E	5	Unknown	9/27/2006	N/A
No common name (Thelypteris verecunda)	4	7/2/1993	1/17/1995	F	1/17/1995	19	N/A	N/A	E	5	Unknown	9/27/2006	N/A
No common name (Thelypteris yaucoensis)	4	7/2/1993	1/17/1995	F	1/17/1995	19	N/A	N/A	E	5	Unknown	9/27/2006	N/A
Pauoa (Ctenitis squamigera)	1	9/26/1994	4/10/1998	F	4/10/1998	23	4,742,000	15	E	5	Stable	3/8/2007	N/A

*Earlier drafts and final plans for some individual species may have become incorporated into later multi-species or ecosystem plans.

www.fws.gov/endangered

GENERAL SPECIES INFORMATION					RECOVERY PLAN INFORMATION					SPECIES/RECOVERY STATUS			
Species Name	Lead Region	Date Listed	Date of First Final Plan	Plan Status*	Date of Current or Active Plan	Number of Actions Implemented	Estimated Costs for Recovery	Estimated Time to Recovery (years)	Listing Classification	Recovery Priority Number	FY 2008 Species' Status	Date 5-Year Status Review Initiated	Date 5-Year Status Review Completed
Quillwort, black spored (Isoetes melanospora)	4	2/5/1988	7/7/1993	F	7/7/1993	10	N/A	N/A	E	5	Decreasing	7/26/2005	9/30/2008
Quillwort, Louisiana (Isoetes louisianensis)	4	10/28/1992	9/30/1996	F	9/30/1996	10	N/A	N/A	E	14	Stable	N/A	N/A
Quillwort, mat-forming (Isoetes tegetiformans)	4	2/5/1988	7/7/1993	F	7/7/1993	10	N/A	N/A	E	8	Decreasing	7/26/2005	9/30/2008
Wawae'iole (Huperzia mannii)	1	5/15/1992	7/29/1997	F	7/29/1997	41	N/A	N/A	E	2	Stable	N/A	N/A
Wawae'iole (Lycopodium (=Phlegmariurus) nutans)	1	3/28/1994	8/10/1998	F	8/10/1998	28	N/A	N/A	E	5	Decreasing	3/8/2007	N/A
Fishes													
Catfish, Yaqui (Ictalurus pricei)	2	8/31/1984	3/29/1995	F	3/29/1995	33	N/A	N/A	T	8	Stable	3/20/2008	N/A
Cavefish, Alabama (Speoplatyrhinus poulsoni)	4	10/11/1977	9/16/1982	RF(2)	10/25/1990	16	N/A	N/A	E	1	Stable	9/8/2006	N/A
Cavefish, Ozark (Amblyopsis rosae)	4	11/1/1984	12/17/1986	F	12/17/1986	10	N/A	N/A	T	8	Stable	9/8/2006	N/A
Chub, bonytail (Gila elegans)	6	4/23/1980	5/16/1984	RF(2)	8/1/2002	54	N/A	N/A	E	5C	Improving	4/18/2007	N/A
Chub, Borax Lake (Gila boraxobius)	1	5/28/1980	2/4/1987	F	2/4/1987	21	N/A	N/A	E	2	Stable	4/11/2006	N/A
Chub, Chihuahua (Gila nigrescens)	2	10/11/1983	4/14/1986	F	4/14/1986	12	N/A	N/A	T	2	Stable	9/21/2007	N/A
Chub, Gila (Gila intermedia)	2	11/2/2005	N/A	N/A	N/A	N/A	N/A	N/A	E	2C	Stable	N/A	N/A
Chub, humpback (Gila cypha)	6	3/11/1967	8/22/1979	RF(2)	9/19/1990	36	N/A	N/A	E	2C	Stable	4/18/2007	N/A
Chub, Hutton tui (Gila bicolor ssp.)	1	3/28/1985	4/27/1998	F	4/27/1998	30	4,200,000	10	T	15	Stable	4/11/2006	2/12/2008
Chub, Mohave tui (Gila bicolor mohavensis)	8	10/13/1970	9/12/1984	F	9/12/1984	49	N/A	N/A	E	6	Stable	3/5/2008	N/A
Chub, Oregon (Oregonichthys crameri)	1	10/18/1993	9/3/1998	F	9/3/1998	77	N/A	N/A	E	8	Improving	3/8/2007	2/11/2008
Chub, Owens tui (Gila bicolor snyderi)	8	8/5/1985	9/30/1998	F	9/30/1998	100	N/A	N/A	E	9	Unknown	3/5/2008	N/A
Chub, Pahranagat roundtail (Gila robusta jordani)	8	10/13/1970	5/26/1998	F	5/26/1998	12	N/A	N/A	E	3C	Decreasing	3/5/2008	N/A
Chub, slender (Erimystax cahni)	4	10/11/1977	7/29/1983	F	7/29/1983	16	N/A	N/A	T	5	Unknown	7/29/2008	N/A
Chub, Sonora (Gila ditaenia)	2	4/30/1986	9/30/1992	F	9/30/1992	22	N/A	N/A	T	2C	Stable	3/20/2008	N/A
Chub, spotfin (Erimonax monachus)	4	10/11/1977	11/21/1983	F	11/21/1983	16	N/A	N/A	T	11	Improving	N/A	N/A
Chub, Virgin River (Gila seminuda (=robusta))	6	8/24/1989	7/9/1979	RF(2)	4/19/1995	40	N/A	N/A	E	2C	Decreasing	4/7/2006	3/26/2008
Chub, Yaqui (Gila purpurea)	2	8/31/1984	3/29/1995	F	3/29/1995	33	N/A	N/A	E	5	Stable	3/20/2008	N/A
Cui-ui (Chasmistes cujus)	8	3/11/1967	1/23/1978	RF(2)	5/15/1992	44	13,959,000	25	E	14	Stable	N/A	N/A
Dace, Ash Meadows speckled (Rhinichthys osculus nevadensis)	8	5/10/1982	9/28/1990	F	9/28/1990	82	N/A	N/A	E	9	Stable	7/29/2008	N/A
Dace, blackside (Phoxinus cumberlandensis)	4	6/12/1987	8/17/1988	F	8/17/1988	11	N/A	N/A	T	11	Stable	7/29/2008	N/A
Dace, Clover Valley speckled (Rhinichthys osculus oligoporus)	8	10/10/1989	5/12/1998	F	5/12/1998	11	N/A	N/A	E	9C	Unknown	2/14/2007	N/A
Dace, desert (Eremichthys acros)	8	3/11/1967	5/27/1997	F	5/27/1997	6	N/A	N/A	T	7C	Stable	3/22/2006	N/A
Dace, Foskett speckled (Rhinichthys osculus ssp.)	1	3/28/1985	4/27/1998	F	4/27/1998	30	4,200,000	10	T	15	Stable	4/11/2006	N/A
Dace, Independence Valley speckled (Rhinichthys osculus lethoporus)	8	10/10/1989	5/12/1998	F	5/12/1998	11	N/A	N/A	E	9C	Unknown	2/14/2007	7/10/2008

*Earlier drafts and final plans for some individual species may have become incorporated into later multi-species or ecosystem plans.

www.fws.gov/endangered

GENERAL SPECIES INFORMATION					RECOVERY PLAN INFORMATION				SPECIES/RECOVERY STATUS				
Species Name	Lead Region	Date Listed	Date of First Final Plan	Plan Status*	Date of Current or Active Plan	Number of Actions Implemented	Estimated Costs for Recovery	Estimated Time to Recovery (years)	Listing Classification	Recovery Priority Number	FY 2008 Species' Status	Date 5-Year Status Review Initiated	Date 5-Year Status Review Completed
Dace, Kendall Warm Springs (Rhinichthys osculus thermalis)	6	10/13/1970	7/12/1982	F	7/12/1982	22	N/A	N/A	E	12C	Decreasing	9/20/2006	10/10/2007
Dace, Moapa (Moapa coriacea)	8	3/11/1967	2/14/1983	RF(1)	5/16/1996	6	N/A	N/A	E	1	Decreasing	N/A	N/A
Darter, amber (Percina antesella)	4	8/5/1985	6/20/1986	F	6/20/1986	11	N/A	N/A	E	5	Unknown	N/A	N/A
Darter, bayou (Etheostoma rubrum)	4	10/28/1975	9/8/1983	RF(1)	7/10/1990	23	226,420	20	T	8C	Stable	9/8/2006	N/A
Darter, bluemask (=jewel) (Etheostoma sp.)	4	12/27/1993	7/25/1997	F	7/25/1997	11	N/A	N/A	E	5	Stable	N/A	N/A
Darter, boulder (Etheostoma wapiti)	4	9/1/1988	7/27/1989	F	7/27/1989	10	N/A	N/A	E	5	Unknown	9/21/2007	N/A
Darter, Cherokee (Etheostoma scotti)	4	12/20/1994	11/17/2000	F	11/17/2000	29	N/A	N/A	T	2C	Unknown	N/A	N/A
Darter, duskytail (Etheostoma percnurum)	4	4/27/1993	3/30/1994	F	3/30/1994	11	N/A	N/A	E	2	Stable	7/28/2006	N/A
Darter, Etowah (Etheostoma etowahae)	4	12/20/1994	11/17/2000	F	11/17/2000	29	N/A	N/A	E	2	Unknown	N/A	N/A
Darter, fountain (E heostoma fonticola)	2	10/13/1970	4/8/1985	RF(1)	2/14/1996	36	N/A	N/A	E	2C	Stable	3/20/2008	N/A
Darter, goldline (Percina aurolineata)	4	4/22/1992	11/17/2000	F	11/17/2000	29	N/A	N/A	T	8	Stable	8/2/2007	N/A
Darter, leopard (Percina pantherina)	2	2/27/1978	9/20/1984	RD(1)	5/3/1993	17	N/A	N/A	T	11C	Stable	4/21/2006	N/A
Darter, Maryland (Etheostoma sellare)	5	3/11/1967	2/2/1982	F	2/2/1982	28	N/A	N/A	E	5	Unknown	1/29/2007	10/5/2007
Darter, Niangua (Etheostoma nianguae)	3	6/12/1985	7/17/1989	F	7/17/1989	11	N/A	N/A	T	8	Stable	10/4/2007	N/A
Darter, Okaloosa (Etheostoma okaloosae)	4	6/4/1973	10/23/1981	RF(1)	10/26/1998	29	N/A	N/A	E	11	Stable	6/21/2005	7/2/2007
Darter, relict (Etheostoma chienense)	4	12/27/1993	N/A	D	7/31/1994	11	N/A	N/A	E	5	Stable	9/21/2007	N/A
Darter, slackwater (Etheostoma boschungi)	4	10/11/1977	3/8/1984	F	3/8/1984	12	N/A	N/A	T	8	Decreasing	8/10/2005	6/24/2008
Darter, snail (Percina tanasi)	4	11/10/1975	5/5/1983	F	5/5/1983	17	N/A	N/A	T	11	Stable	7/28/2006	N/A
Darter, vermilion (Etheostoma chermocki)	4	11/28/2001	8/6/2007	F	8/6/2007	17	N/A	N/A	E	2	Stable	7/29/2008	N/A
Darter, watercress (Etheostoma nuchale)	4	10/13/1970	6/25/1980	RF(2)	3/29/1993	12	N/A	N/A	E	2	Improving	6/14/2005	N/A
Gambusia, Big Bend (Gambusia gaigei)	2	3/11/1967	9/19/1984	F	9/19/1984	16	N/A	N/A	E	2	Stable	3/20/2008	N/A
Gambusia, Clear Creek (Gambusia heterochir)	2	3/11/1967	1/14/1982	F	1/14/1982	33	N/A	N/A	E	2	Stable	3/20/2008	N/A
Gambusia, Pecos (Gambusia nobilis)	2	10/13/1970	5/9/1985	F	5/9/1985	20	N/A	N/A	E	2	Stable	N/A	N/A
Gambusia, San Marcos (Gambusia geongei)	2	7/14/1980	4/8/1985	RF(1)	2/14/1996	36	N/A	N/A	E	2C	Presumed Extinct	3/20/2008	N/A
Goby, tidewater (Eucyclogobius newberryi)	8	2/4/1994	1/23/2006	F	12/7/2005	34	N/A	N/A	E	7C	Stable	3/22/2006	9/28/2007
Logperch, Conasauga (Percina jenkinsi)	4	8/5/1985	6/20/1986	F	6/20/1986	11	N/A	N/A	E	5	Unknown	7/26/2005	N/A
Logperch, Roanoke (Percina rex)	5	8/18/1989	3/20/1992	F	3/20/1992	13	N/A	N/A	E	5C	Improving	6/1/2006	9/19/2007
Madtom, Neosho (Noturus placidus)	6	5/22/1990	9/30/1991	F	9/30/1991	35	412,000	5	T	8C	Unknown	N/A	N/A
Madtom, pygmy (Noturus stanauli)	4	4/27/1993	9/27/1994	F	9/27/1994	11	N/A	N/A	E	5	Stable	7/29/2008	N/A
Madtom, Scioto (Noturus trautmani)	3	10/28/1975	N/A	E	N/A	N/A	N/A	N/A	E	5	Extinct	N/A	N/A
Madtom, smoky (Noturus baileyi)	4	10/26/1984	8/9/1985	F	8/9/1985	11	N/A	N/A	E	8	Stable	7/28/2006	N/A

*Earlier drafts and final plans for some individual species may have become incorporated into later multi-species or ecosystem plans.

www.fws.gov/endangered

	GENERAL SPECIES INFORMATION				RECOVERY PLAN INFORMATION				SPECIES/RECOVERY STATUS				
Species Name	Lead Region	Date Listed	Date of First Final Plan	Plan Status*	Date of Current or Active Plan	Number of Actions Implemented	Estimated Costs for Recovery	Estimated Time to Recovery (years)	Listing Classifi-cation	Recovery Priority Number	FY 2008 Species' Status	Date 5-Year Status Review Initiated	Date 5-Year Status Review Completed
Madtom, yellowfin (Noturus flavipinnis)	4	10/11/1977	6/23/1983	F	6/23/1983	16	N/A	N/A	T	8	Stable	7/28/2006	N/A
Minnow, Devils River (Dionda diaboli)	2	10/20/1999	9/13/2005	F	9/13/2005	38	2,920,000	9	T	2	Stable	4/23/2007	9/11/2008
Minnow, loach (Tiaroga cobitis)	2	10/28/1986	9/30/1991	F	9/30/1991	33	N/A	N/A	T	4C	Decreasing	4/23/2007	N/A
Minnow, Rio Grande silvery (Hybognathus amarus)	2	7/20/1994	7/8/1999	RD(1)	1/18/2007	69	114,125,000	30	E	2C	Improving	N/A	N/A
Pikeminnow (=squawfish), Colorado (Ptychocheilus lucius)	6	3/11/1967	3/16/1978	RF(2)	8/28/2002	33	N/A	N/A	E	8C	Stable	4/18/2007	N/A
Poolfish, Pahrump (Empetrichthys latos)	8	3/11/1967	3/17/1980	F	3/17/1980	58	N/A	N/A	E	11	Decreasing	3/22/2006	N/A
Pupfish, Ash Meadows Amargosa (Cyprinodon nevadensis mionectes)	8	5/10/1982	9/28/1990	F	9/28/1990	82	N/A	N/A	E	15	Stable	3/22/2006	N/A
Pupfish, Comanche Springs (Cyprinodon elegans)	2	3/11/1967	9/2/1981	F	9/2/1981	19	N/A	N/A	E	2	Decreasing	N/A	N/A
Pupfish, desert (Cyprinodon macularius)	2	3/31/1986	12/8/1993	F	12/8/1993	11	N/A	N/A	E	2C	Improving	4/21/2006	N/A
Pupfish, Devils Hole (Cyprinodon diabolis)	8	3/11/1967	9/28/1990	F	9/28/1990	82	N/A	N/A	E	5	Stable	N/A	N/A
Pupfish, Leon Springs (Cyprinodon bovinus)	2	8/15/1980	8/14/1985	F	8/14/1985	19	N/A	N/A	E	2	Stable	3/20/2008	N/A
Pupfish, Owens (Cyprinodon radiosus)	8	3/11/1967	9/30/1998	F	9/30/1998	100	N/A	N/A	E	2	Decreasing	3/5/2008	N/A
Pupfish, Warm Springs (Cyprinodon nevadensis pectoralis)	8	10/13/1970	9/28/1990	F	9/28/1990	82	N/A	N/A	E	9	Stable	N/A	N/A
Salmon, Atlantic (Salmo salar)	5	11/17/2000	12/20/2005	F	4/7/2006	160	N/A	N/A	E	6C	Decreasing	N/A	N/A
Sculpin, pygmy (Cottus paulus (=pygmaeus))	4	9/28/1989	8/6/1991	F	8/6/1991	10	N/A	N/A	T	8	Stable	6/14/2005	7/28/2008
Shiner, Arkansas River (Notropis girardi)	2	11/23/1998	N/A	D	9/12/2008	13	N/A	N/A	T	5C	Decreasing	N/A	N/A
Shiner, beautiful (Cyprinella formosa)	2	8/31/1984	3/29/1995	F	3/29/1995	33	N/A	N/A	T	2	Stable	3/20/2008	N/A
Shiner, blue (Cyprinella caerulea)	4	4/22/1992	8/30/1995	F	8/30/1995	11	N/A	N/A	T	8	Stable	8/2/2007	N/A
Shiner, Cahaba (Notropis cahabae)	4	10/25/1990	4/23/1992	F	4/23/1992	4	N/A	N/A	E	2	Improving	N/A	N/A
Shiner, Cape Fear (Notropis mekistocholas)	4	9/25/1987	10/7/1988	F	10/7/1988	10	N/A	N/A	E	5	Stable	N/A	N/A
Shiner, palezone (Notropis albizonatus)	4	4/27/1993	7/7/1997	F	7/7/1997	11	N/A	N/A	E	5	Stable	7/29/2008	N/A
Shiner, Pecos bluntnose (Notropis simus pecosensis)	2	2/20/1987	9/30/1992	F	9/30/1992	23	N/A	N/A	T	3	Improving	4/21/2006	N/A
Shiner, Topeka (Notropis topeka (=tristis))	6	12/15/1998	N/A	N/A	N/A	N/A	N/A	N/A	E	8C	Stable	12/8/2004	N/A
Silverside, Waccamaw (Menidia extensa)	4	4/8/1987	8/11/1993	F	8/11/1993	13	N/A	N/A	T	8	Stable	N/A	N/A
Smelt, delta (Hypomesus transpacificus)	8	3/5/1993	11/26/1996	F	11/26/1996	74	N/A	N/A	T	2C	Stable	8/1/2003	3/31/2004
Spikedace (Meda fulgida)	2	7/1/1986	9/30/1991	F	9/30/1991	34	N/A	N/A	T	4C	Decreasing	4/23/2007	N/A
Spinedace, Big Spring (Lepidomeda mollispinis pratensis)	8	3/28/1985	1/20/1994	F	1/20/1994	26	196,000	13	T	3	Unknown	N/A	N/A
Spinedace, Little Colorado (Lepidomeda vittata)	2	3/11/1967	1/9/1998	F	1/9/1998	46	2,405,000	10	T	5C	Decreasing	1/11/2006	N/A

*Earlier drafts and final plans for some individual species may have become incorporated into later multi-species or ecosystem plans.

GENERAL SPECIES INFORMATION					RECOVERY PLAN INFORMATION					SPECIES/RECOVERY STATUS			
Species Name	Lead Region	Date Listed	Date of First Final Plan	Plan Status*	Date of Current or Active Plan	Number of Actions Implemented	Estimated Costs for Recovery	Estimated Time to Recovery (years)	Listing Classification	Recovery Priority Number	FY 2008 Species' Status	Date 5-Year Status Review Initiated	Date 5-Year Status Review Completed
Spinedace, White River (Lepidomeda albivallis)	8	9/12/1985	3/28/1994	F	3/28/1994	19	N/A	N/A	E	2C	Stable	3/22/2006	N/A
Springfish, Hiko White River (Crenichthys baileyi grandis)	8	9/27/1985	5/26/1998	F	5/26/1998	12	N/A	N/A	E	3C	Unknown	2/14/2007	N/A
Springfish, Railroad Valley (Crenichthys nevadae)	8	3/31/1986	3/15/1997	F	3/15/1997	12	570,000	7	T	2C	Stable	2/14/2007	N/A
Springfish, White River (Crenichthys baileyi baileyi)	8	9/27/1985	5/26/1998	F	5/26/1998	12	N/A	N/A	E	3C	Stable	2/14/2007	N/A
Stickleback, unarmored threespine (Gasterosteus aculeatus williamsoni)	8	10/13/1970	12/27/1977	RF(1)	12/26/1985	39	N/A	N/A	E	3	Decreasing	3/5/2008	N/A
Sturgeon, Alabama (Scaphirhynchus suttkusi)	4	5/5/2000	N/A	N/A	N/A	N/A	N/A	N/A	E	5	Unknown	N/A	N/A
Sturgeon, gulf (Acipenser oxyrinchus desotoi)	4	9/30/1991	9/22/1995	F	9/22/1995	37	N/A	N/A	T	12	Stable	4/16/2008	N/A
Sturgeon, pallid (Scaphirhynchus albus)	6	9/6/1990	11/7/1993	F	11/7/1993	61	N/A	N/A	E	2C	Improving	7/7/2005	6/13/2007
Sturgeon, white (Acipenser transmontanus)	1	9/6/1994	9/30/1999	F	9/30/1999	54	N/A	N/A	E	3C	Decreasing	N/A	N/A
Sucker, June (Chasmistes liorus)	6	3/31/1986	6/25/1999	F	6/25/1999	58	50,000,000	40	E	5C	Improving	7/21/2004	7/19/2007
Sucker, Lost River (Deltistes luxatus)	8	7/18/1988	3/17/1993	F	3/17/1993	85	N/A	N/A	E	4C	Improving	7/21/2004	7/19/2007
Sucker, Modoc (Catostomus microps)	8	6/11/1985	N/A	E	N/A	35	N/A	N/A	E	14	Unknown	3/22/2006	N/A
Sucker, razorback (Xyrauchen texanus)	6	10/23/1991	12/23/1998	RF(1)	8/28/2002	55	N/A	N/A	E	1C	Improving	4/18/2007	N/A
Sucker, Santa Ana (Catostomus santaanae)	8	4/12/2000	N/A	N/A	N/A	N/A	N/A	N/A	T	5C	Unknown	N/A	N/A
Sucker, shortnose (Chasmistes brevirostris)	8	7/18/1988	3/17/1993	F	3/17/1993	85	N/A	N/A	E	4C	Decreasing	7/21/2004	7/19/2007
Sucker, Warner (Catostomus warnerensis)	1	9/27/1985	4/27/1998	F	4/27/1998	30	4,200,000	10	T	2C	Unknown	4/11/2006	N/A
Topminnow, Gila (Poeciliopsis occidentalis)	2	3/11/1967	3/15/1984	RD(1)	3/5/1999	N/A	3,397,000	20	E	3C	Improving	4/23/2007	N/A
Trout, Apache (Oncorhynchus apache)	2	3/11/1967	8/20/1979	RD(2)	7/27/2007	11	N/A	N/A	T	14C	Improving	4/21/2006	N/A
Trout, bull (Salvelinus confluentus)	1	6/10/1998	N/A	D	7/1/2004	1670	N/A	N/A	T	9C	Stable	4/13/2004	4/25/2008
Trout, Gila (Oncorhynchus gilae)	2	3/11/1967	1/12/1979	RF(3)	9/10/2003	14	2,839,000	13	T	8	Stable	N/A	N/A
Trout, greenback cut hroat (Oncorhynchus clarki stomias)	6	3/11/1967	11/11/1977	RF(2)	3/1/1998	37	634,000	5	T	15	Stable	12/14/2005	N/A
Trout, Lahontan cutthroat (Oncorhynchus clarki henshawi)	8	10/13/1970	1/30/1995	F	1/30/1995	117	N/A	N/A	T	3C	Decreasing	7/1/2007	N/A
Trout, Little Kern golden (Oncorhynchus aguabonita whitei)	8	5/15/1978	N/A	E	N/A	N/A	N/A	N/A	T	9	Stable	N/A	N/A
Trout, Paiute cutthroat (Oncorhynchus clarki seleniris)	8	3/11/1967	1/25/1985	RF(1)	9/10/2004	42	N/A	N/A	T	9	Stable	3/22/2006	7/10/2008
Woundfin (Plagopterus argentissimus)	6	10/13/1970	7/9/1979	RF(2)	4/19/1995	40	N/A	N/A	E	1C	Decreasing	4/7/2006	3/28/2008
Flowering Plants													
'Ahinahina (Argyroxiphium sandwicense ssp. macrocephalum)	1	5/15/1992	7/29/1997	F	7/29/1997	41	N/A	N/A	T	9	Decreasing	N/A	N/A

*Earlier drafts and final plans for some individual species may have become incorporated into later multi-species or ecosystem plans.

www.fws.gov/endangered

	GENERAL SPECIES INFORMATION			RECOVERY PLAN INFORMATION						SPECIES/RECOVERY STATUS			
Species Name	Lead Region	Date Listed	Date of First Final Plan	Plan Status*	Date of Current or Active Plan	Number of Actions Implemented	Estimated Costs for Recovery	Estimated Time to Recovery (years)	Listing Classifi- cation	Recovery Priority Number	FY 2008 Species' Status	Date 5-Year Status Review Initiated	Date 5-Year Status Review Completed
'Ahinahina (Argyroxiphium sandwicense ssp. sandwicense)	1	3/21/1986	9/30/1993	F	9/30/1993	31	N/A	N/A	E	6	Stable	N/A	N/A
'Aiakeakua, popolo (Solanum sandwicense)	1	2/25/1994	9/20/1995	F	9/20/1995	89	N/A	N/A	E	2	Decreasing	3/8/2007	N/A
'Aiea (Nothocestrum breviflorum)	1	3/4/1994	9/26/1996	F	9/26/1996	78	9,395,000	20	E	5	Stable	N/A	N/A
'Aiea (Nothocestrum peltatum)	1	2/25/1994	9/20/1995	F	9/20/1995	89	N/A	N/A	E	5	Stable	3/8/2007	N/A
'Akoko (Chamaesyce celastroides var. kaenana)	1	10/29/1991	8/10/1998	F	8/10/1998	28	N/A	N/A	E	9	Stable	7/6/2005	8/2/2007
'Akoko (Chamaesyce deppeana)	1	3/28/1994	8/10/1998	F	8/10/1998	28	N/A	N/A	E	5	Decreasing	7/6/2005	8/2/2007
'Akoko (Chamaesyce herbs ii)	1	10/10/1996	8/10/1998	F	8/10/1998	28	N/A	N/A	E	8	Stable	7/6/2005	8/2/2007
'Akoko (Chamaesyce kuwaleana)	1	10/29/1991	8/10/1998	F	8/10/1998	28	N/A	N/A	E	8	Decreasing	N/A	N/A
'Akoko (Chamaesyce rockii)	1	10/10/1996	8/10/1998	F	8/10/1998	28	N/A	N/A	E	8	Decreasing	N/A	N/A
'Akoko (Euphorbia haeleeleana)	1	10/10/1996	7/10/1999	F	7/10/1999	56	33,900,000	11	E	5	Decreasing	4/29/2008	N/A
'Akoko, Ewa Plains (Chamaesyce skottsbergii var. kalaeloana)	1	8/24/1982	N/A	D	10/5/1993	50	N/A	N/A	E	6	Stable	7/6/2005	8/2/2007
'Anaunau (Lepidium arbuscula)	1	10/10/1996	8/10/1998	F	8/10/1998	28	N/A	N/A	E	8	Decreasing	3/8/2007	N/A
'Anunu (Sicyos alba)	1	10/10/1996	5/11/1998	F	9/26/1996	78	9,395,000	20	E	2	Decreasing	N/A	N/A
'Awikiwiki (Canavalia molokaiensis)	1	10/8/1992	9/26/1996	F	9/26/1996	29	24,784,000	21	E	2	Decreasing	N/A	N/A
'Oha wai (Clermontia drepanomorpha)	1	10/10/1996	5/11/1998	F	9/26/1996	78	9,395,000	20	E	2	Decreasing	N/A	N/A
'Oha wai (Clermontia lindseyana)	1	3/4/1994	9/26/1996	F	9/26/1996	78	9,395,000	20	E	2	Stable	4/29/2008	N/A
'Oha wai (Clermontia oblongifolia ssp. brevipes)	1	10/8/1992	9/26/1996	F	9/26/1996	29	24,784,000	21	E	6	Decreasing	N/A	N/A
'Oha wai (Clermontia oblongifolia ssp. mauiensis)	1	5/15/1992	7/29/1997	F	7/29/1997	41	N/A	N/A	E	6	Decreasing	N/A	N/A
'Oha wai (Clermontia peleana)	1	3/4/1994	9/26/1996	F	9/26/1996	78	9,395,000	20	E	5	Stable	4/11/2006	1/18/2008
'Oha wai (Clermontia pyrularia)	1	3/4/1994	9/26/1996	F	9/26/1996	78	9,395,000	20	E	2	Decreasing	7/6/2005	8/2/2007
'Oha wai (Clermontia samuelii)	1	9/3/1999	9/19/2002	F	7/10/1999	56	33,900,000	11	E	5	Decreasing	N/A	N/A
'Ohe'ohe (Tetraplasandra gymnocarpa)	1	3/28/1994	8/10/1998	F	8/10/1998	28	N/A	N/A	E	5	Decreasing	N/A	N/A
A'e (Zanthoxylum dipetalum var. tomentosum)	1	10/10/1998	5/11/1998	F	9/26/1996	78	9,395,000	20	E	6	Decreasing	3/8/2007	N/A
A'e (Zanthoxylum hawaiiense)	1	3/4/1994	9/26/1996	F	9/26/1996	78	9,395,000	20	E	2	Decreasing	4/29/2008	N/A
Alani (Melicope adscendens)	1	12/5/1994	7/29/1997	F	7/29/1997	41	N/A	N/A	E	5	Stable	4/11/2006	1/18/2008
Alani (Melicope balloui)	1	12/5/1994	7/29/1997	F	7/29/1997	41	N/A	N/A	E	5	Decreasing	N/A	N/A
Alani (Melicope haupuensis)	1	2/25/1994	9/20/1995	F	9/20/1995	89	N/A	N/A	E	5	Decreasing	3/8/2007	N/A
Alani (Melicope knudsenii)	1	2/25/1994	9/20/1995	F	9/20/1995	89	N/A	N/A	E	5	Stable	3/8/2007	N/A
Alani (Melicope lydgatei)	1	3/28/1994	8/10/1998	F	8/10/1998	28	N/A	N/A	E	5	Decreasing	3/8/2007	N/A
Alani (Melicope mucronulata)	1	5/15/1992	7/29/1997	F	7/29/1997	41	N/A	N/A	E	5	Stable	4/11/2006	1/18/2008
Alani (Melicope munroi)	1	9/3/1999	9/19/2002	F	7/10/1999	56	33,900,000	11	E	5	Decreasing	N/A	N/A
Alani (Melicope ovalis)	1	12/5/1994	7/29/1997	F	7/29/1997	41	N/A	N/A	E	5	Decreasing	N/A	N/A
Alani (Melicope pallida)	1	2/25/1994	9/20/1995	F	9/20/1995	89	N/A	N/A	E	5	Decreasing	4/29/2008	N/A
Alani (Melicope quadrangularis)	1	2/25/1994	9/20/1995	F	9/20/1995	89	N/A	N/A	E	5	Decreasing	4/29/2008	N/A
Alani (Melicope reflexa)	1	10/8/1992	9/26/1996	F	9/26/1996	29	24,784,000	21	E	8	Decreasing	N/A	N/A
Alani (Melicope saint-johnii)	1	10/10/1996	8/10/1998	F	8/10/1998	28	N/A	N/A	E	8	Decreasing	N/A	N/A
Alani (Melicope zahlbruckneri)	1	10/10/1996	5/11/1998	F	9/26/1996	78	9,395,000	20	E	2	Decreasing	4/11/2006	1/18/2008

*Earlier drafts and final plans for some individual species may have become incorporated into later multi-species or ecosystem plans.

www.fws.gov/endangered

GENERAL SPECIES INFORMATION			RECOVERY PLAN INFORMATION						SPECIES/RECOVERY STATUS				
Species Name	Lead Region	Date Listed	Date of First Final Plan	Plan Status*	Date of Current or Active Plan	Number of Actions Implemented	Estimated Costs for Recovery	Estimated Time to Recovery (years)	Listing Classification	Recovery Priority Number	FY 2008 Species' Status	Date 5-Year Status Review Initiated	Date 5-Year Status Review Completed
Allocarya, Calistoga (Plagiobo hrys strictus)	8	10/22/1997	N/A	N/A	N/A	N/A	N/A	N/A	E	2C	Unknown	3/5/2008	N/A
Alopecurus, Sonoma (Alopecurus aequalis var. sonomensis)	8	10/22/1997	N/A	N/A	N/A	N/A	N/A	N/A	E	9	Unknown	N/A	N/A
Amaranth, seabeach (Amaranthus pumilus)	4	4/7/1993	11/12/1996	F	11/12/1996	11	N/A	N/A	T	8C	Decreasing	9/20/2005	7/19/2007
Ambrosia, San Diego (Ambrosia pumila)	8	7/2/2002	N/A	N/A	N/A	N/A	N/A	N/A	E	5	Decreasing	N/A	N/A
Ambrosia, south Texas (Ambrosia cheiranthifolia)	2	8/24/1994	N/A	N/A	N/A	N/A	N/A	N/A	E	8	Stable	3/20/2008	N/A
Amole, purple (Chlorogalum purpureum)	8	3/20/2000	N/A	N/A	N/A	N/A	N/A	N/A	T	8	Stable	2/14/2007	9/30/2008
Amphianthus, little (Amphianthus pusillus)	4	2/5/1988	7/7/1993	F	7/7/1993	10	N/A	N/A	T	13	Decreasing	7/26/2005	9/30/2008
Arrowhead, bunched (Sagittaria fasciculata)	4	8/31/1979	9/8/1983	F	9/8/1983	13	N/A	N/A	E	2C	Unknown	N/A	N/A
Aster, decurrent false (Boltonia decurrens)	3	11/14/1988	9/28/1990	F	9/28/1990	29	58,100	7	T	8	Decreasing	3/30/2006	N/A
Aster, Florida golden (Chrysopsis floridana)	4	5/16/1986	8/29/1988	F	8/29/1988	13	N/A	N/A	E	5	Improving	4/16/2008	N/A
Aster, Ruth's golden (Pityopsis ruthii)	4	7/18/1985	6/11/1992	F	6/11/1992	18	162,500	6	E	5C	Stable	7/28/2006	N/A
Aupaka (Isodendrion hosakae)	1	1/14/1991	5/23/1994	F	5/23/1994	38	N/A	N/A	E	5	Decreasing	N/A	N/A
Aupaka (Isodendrion laurifolium)	1	10/10/1996	7/10/1999	F	7/10/1999	56	33,900,000	11	E	8	Decreasing	3/8/2007	N/A
Aupaka (Isodendrion longifolium)	1	10/10/1996	7/10/1999	F	7/10/1999	56	33,900,000	11	T	8	Decreasing	N/A	N/A
Avens, spreading (Geum radiatum)	4	4/5/1990	4/28/1993	F	4/28/1993	16	N/A	N/A	E	2	Stable	7/29/2008	N/A
Awiwi (Centaurium sebaeoides)	1	10/29/1991	7/10/1999	F	7/10/1999	56	33,900,000	11	E	2	Decreasing	4/29/2008	N/A
Awiwi (Hedyotis cookiana)	1	2/25/1994	9/20/1995	F	9/20/1995	89	N/A	N/A	E	5	Decreasing	4/29/2008	N/A
Ayenia, Texas (Ayenia limitaris)	2	8/24/1994	N/A	N/A	N/A	N/A	N/A	N/A	E	5	Decreasing	3/20/2008	N/A
Baccharis, Encinitas (Baccharis vanessae)	8	10/7/1996	N/A	N/A	N/A	N/A	N/A	N/A	T	5C	Decreasing	N/A	N/A
Barberry, island (Berberis pinnata ssp. insularis)	8	7/31/1997	9/26/2000	F	9/26/2000	28	51,920,000	40	E	6	Decreasing	2/14/2007	7/10/2008
Barberry, Nevin's (Berberis nevinii)	8	10/13/1998	N/A	N/A	N/A	N/A	N/A	N/A	E	2	Decreasing	3/5/2008	N/A
Bariaco (Trichilia triacantha)	4	2/5/1988	8/20/1991	F	8/20/1991	21	N/A	N/A	E	11	Stable	N/A	N/A
Beaked-rush, Knieskern's (Rhynchospora knieskernii)	5	7/18/1991	9/29/1993	F	9/29/1993	15	78,000	4	T	14	Unknown	1/29/2007	8/27/2008
Beardtongue, Penland (Penstemon penlandii)	6	7/13/1989	9/30/1992	F	9/30/1992	13	N/A	N/A	E	14	Stable	N/A	N/A
Beargrass, Britton's (Nolina brittoniana)	4	4/27/1993	6/20/1996	RF(1)	6/20/1996	35	N/A	N/A	E	8	Unknown	N/A	N/A
Bear-poppy, dwarf (Arctomecon humilis)	6	12/6/1979	12/31/1985	F	12/31/1985	22	N/A	N/A	E	5C	Decreasing	N/A	N/A
Beauty, Harper's (Harperocallis flava)	4	11/1/1979	9/14/1983	F	9/14/1983	24	N/A	N/A	E	7	Stable	4/16/2008	N/A
Bedstraw, El Dorado (Galium californicum ssp. sierrae)	8	10/18/1996	8/30/2002	F	8/30/2002	52	N/A	N/A	E	6C	Stable	N/A	N/A
Bedstraw, island (Galium buxifolium)	8	7/31/1997	9/26/2000	F	9/26/2000	28	51,920,000	40	E	2	Stable	N/A	N/A

*Earlier drafts and final plans for some individual species may
have become incorporated into later multi-species or ecosystem plans.

www.fws.gov/endangered

GENERAL SPECIES INFORMATION			RECOVERY PLAN INFORMATION						SPECIES/RECOVERY STATUS				
Species Name	Lead Region	Date Listed	Date of First Final Plan	Plan Status*	Date of Current or Active Plan	Number of Actions Implemented	Estimated Costs for Recovery	Estimated Time to Recovery (years)	Listing Classification	Recovery Priority Number	FY 2008 Species' Status	Date 5-Year Status Review Initiated	Date 5-Year Status Review Completed
Bellflower, Brooksville (Campanula robinsiae)	4	7/27/1989	6/20/1994	F	6/20/1994	23	N/A	N/A	E	8	Decreasing	N/A	N/A
Birch, Virginia round-leaf (Betula uber)	5	5/27/1978	3/3/1982	RF(2)	9/24/1990	10	321,500	10	T	14	Stable	7/1/2005	10/4/2006
Bird's-beak, palmate-bracted (Cordylanthus palmatus)	8	7/11/1986	9/30/1998	F	9/30/1998	223	N/A	N/A	E	2C	Unknown	2/14/2007	N/A
Bird's-beak, Pennell's (Cordylanthus tenuis ssp. capillaris)	8	2/3/1995	9/30/1998	F	9/30/1998	180	N/A	N/A	E	6	Unknown	N/A	N/A
Bird's-beak, salt marsh (Cordylanthus maritimus ssp. maritimus)	8	10/29/1978	12/6/1985	F	12/6/1985	78	N/A	N/A	E	6	Unknown	2/14/2007	N/A
Bird's-beak, soft (Cordylanthus mollis ssp. mollis)	8	11/20/1997	N/A	N/A	N/A	N/A	N/A	N/A	E	9C	Unknown	2/14/2007	N/A
Birds-in-a-nest, white (Macbridea alba)	4	5/8/1992	6/22/1994	F	6/22/1994	16	N/A	N/A	T	8	Unknown	4/16/2008	N/A
Bittercress, small-anthered (Cardamine micran hera)	4	9/21/1989	7/10/1991	F	7/10/1991	16	N/A	N/A	E	5	Unknown	7/29/2008	N/A
Bladderpod, Dudley Bluffs (Lesquerella congesta)	6	2/6/1990	8/13/1993	F	8/13/1993	13	N/A	N/A	T	2C	Stable	9/20/2006	6/20/2008
Bladderpod, kodachrome (Lesquerella tumulosa)	6	10/6/1993	N/A	N/A	N/A	N/A	N/A	N/A	E	11	Unknown	N/A	N/A
Bladderpod, lyrate (Lesquerella lyrata)	4	9/28/1990	10/17/1996	F	10/17/1996	10	N/A	N/A	T	8	Decreasing	8/2/2007	N/A
Bladderpod, Missouri (Lesquerella filiformis)	3	1/8/1987	4/7/1988	F	4/7/1988	8	N/A	N/A	T	8	Improving	7/19/2005	1/14/2008
Bladderpod, San Bernardino Mountains (Lesquerella kingii ssp. bernardina)	8	8/24/1994	N/A	D	9/30/1997	22	N/A	N/A	E	9	Stable	3/5/2008	N/A
Bladderpod, Spring Creek (Lesquerella perforata)	4	12/23/1996	9/6/2006	F	9/6/2006	15	6,407,500	20	E	2	Unknown	N/A	N/A
Bladderpod, white (Lesquerella pallida)	2	3/11/1987	10/16/1992	F	10/16/1992	18	N/A	N/A	E	2	Unknown	N/A	N/A
Bladderpod, Zapata (Lesquerella thamnophila)	2	11/22/1999	8/25/2004	F	8/25/2004	21	N/A	N/A	E	5C	Decreasing	N/A	N/A
Blazingstar, Ash Meadows (Mentzelia leucophylla)	8	5/20/1985	9/28/1990	F	9/28/1990	82	N/A	N/A	T	8	Unknown	N/A	N/A
Blazingstar, Heller's (Liatris helleri)	4	11/19/1987	5/1/1989	RF(1)	1/28/2000	18	N/A	N/A	T	8	Unknown	N/A	N/A
Blazingstar, scrub (Liatris ohlingerae)	4	7/27/1989	5/18/1999	F	5/18/1999	1404	N/A	N/A	E	2	Unknown	N/A	N/A
Bluecurls, Hidden Lake (Trichostema austromontanum ssp. compactum)	8	9/14/1998	N/A	N/A	N/A	N/A	N/A	N/A	T	15	Stable	7/7/2005	7/28/2006
Bluegrass, Hawaiian (Poa sandvicensis)	1	5/13/1992	9/20/1995	F	9/20/1995	89	N/A	N/A	E	5	Decreasing	4/29/2008	N/A
Bluegrass, Mann's (Poa mannii)	1	11/10/1994	9/20/1995	F	9/20/1995	89	N/A	N/A	E	5	Decreasing	4/29/2008	N/A
Bluegrass, Napa (Poa napensis)	8	10/22/1997	N/A	N/A	N/A	N/A	N/A	N/A	E	2C	Unknown	3/5/2008	N/A
Bluegrass, San Bernardino (Poa atropurpurea)	8	9/14/1998	N/A	N/A	N/A	N/A	N/A	N/A	E	2	Unknown	2/14/2007	9/30/2008
Blue-star, Kearney's (Amsonia kearneyana)	2	1/19/1989	5/24/1993	F	5/24/1993	22	N/A	N/A	E	2	Unknown	3/20/2008	N/A
Bluet, Roan Mountain (Hedyotis purpurea var. montana)	4	4/5/1990	5/13/1996	F	5/13/1996	32	N/A	N/A	E	6	Unknown	7/29/2008	N/A
Bonamia, Florida (Bonamia grandiflora)	4	11/2/1987	1/29/1990	RF(1)	6/20/1996	35	N/A	N/A	T	8	Unknown	4/26/2007	8/28/2008
Boxwood, Vahl's (Buxus vahlii)	4	8/13/1985	4/28/1987	F	4/28/1987	21	N/A	N/A	E	11	Stable	N/A	N/A

*Earlier drafts and final plans for some individual species may have become incorporated into later multi-species or ecosystem plans.

17

www.fws.gov/endangered

Species Name	Lead Region	Date Listed	Date of First Final Plan	Plan Status*	Date of Current or Active Plan	Number of Actions Implemented	Estimated Costs for Recovery	Estimated Time to Recovery (years)	Listing Classification	Recovery Priority Number	FY 2008 Species' Status	Date 5-Year Status Review Initiated	Date 5-Year Status Review Completed
Brodiaea, Chinese Camp (Brodiaea pallida)	8	9/14/1998	N/A	N/A	N/A	N/A	N/A	N/A	T	2C	Stable	7/7/2005	1/10/2008
Brodiaea, thread-leaved (Brodiaea filifolia)	8	10/13/1998	N/A	N/A	N/A	N/A	N/A	N/A	T	2	Decreasing	3/22/2006	N/A
Broom, San Clemente Island (Lotus dendroideus ssp. traskiae)	8	9/12/1977	1/26/1984	F	1/26/1984	54	N/A	N/A	E	15	Stable	7/7/2005	9/24/2007
Buckwheat, cushenbury (Eriogonum ovalifolium var. vineum)	8	8/24/1994	N/A	D	9/30/1997	22	N/A	N/A	E	3C	Unknown	N/A	N/A
Buckwheat, Ione (incl. Irish Hill (Eriogonum apricum (incl. var. prostratum))	8	5/26/1999	N/A	N/A	N/A	N/A	N/A	N/A	E	2C	Unknown	3/5/2008	N/A
Buckwheat, scrub (Eriogonum longifolium var. gnaphalifolium)	4	4/27/1993	6/20/1996	RF(1)	6/20/1996	35	N/A	N/A	T	15	Unknown	4/26/2007	7/23/2008
Buckwheat, steamboat (Eriogonum ovalifolium var. williamsiae)	8	7/8/1986	9/20/1995	F	9/20/1995	15	N/A	N/A	E	6C	Stable	3/22/2006	N/A
Bulrush, Northeastern (Scirpus ancistrochaetus)	5	5/7/1991	8/25/1993	F	8/25/1993	35	N/A	N/A	E	14	Stable	7/6/2005	N/A
Bush-clover, prairie (Lespedeza leptostachya)	3	1/9/1987	10/6/1988	F	10/6/1988	13	N/A	N/A	T	8	Stable	N/A	N/A
Bush-mallow, San Clemente Island (Malacothamnus clementinus)	8	9/12/1977	1/26/1984	F	1/26/1984	54	N/A	N/A	E	14	Stable	7/7/2005	9/28/2007
Bush-mallow, Santa Cruz Island (Malacothamnus fasciculatus var. nesioticus)	8	7/31/1997	9/26/2000	F	9/26/2000	28	51,920,000	40	E	3	Stable	3/22/2006	9/25/2007
Buttercup, autumn (Ranunculus aestivalis (=aciformis))	6	7/21/1989	9/16/1991	F	9/16/1991	22	N/A	N/A	E	5	Improving	N/A	N/A
Butterfly plant, Colorado (Gaura neomexicana var. coloradensis)	6	10/18/2000	N/A	N/A	N/A	N/A	N/A	N/A	T	15	Stable	N/A	N/A
Butterweed, Layne's (Senecio layneae)	8	10/18/1996	8/30/2002	F	8/30/2002	52	N/A	N/A	T	5C	Stable	N/A	N/A
Butterwort, Godfrey's (Pinguicula ionantha)	4	7/12/1993	6/22/1994	F	6/22/1994	16	N/A	N/A	T	14	Unknown	4/16/2008	N/A
Button, Mohr's Barbara (Marshallia mohrii)	4	9/7/1988	11/26/1991	F	11/26/1991	12	N/A	N/A	T	14	Stable	N/A	N/A
Button-celery, San Diego (Eryngium aristulatum var. parishii)	8	8/3/1993	9/3/1998	F	9/3/1998	14	N/A	N/A	E	3C	Unknown	N/A	N/A
Cactus, Arizona hedgehog (Echinocereus triglochidiatus)	2	11/26/1979	N/A	D	9/30/1984	N/A	N/A	N/A	E	3	Unknown	3/20/2008	N/A
Cactus, Bakersfield (Opuntia treleasei)	8	7/19/1990	9/30/1998	F	9/30/1998	223	N/A	N/A	E	3C	Decreasing	3/22/2006	N/A
Cactus, black lace (Echinocereus reichenbachii var. albertii)	2	11/28/1979	3/18/1987	F	3/18/1987	20	N/A	N/A	E	3	Unknown	4/21/2006	N/A
Cactus, Brady pincushion (Pediocactus bradyi)	2	11/26/1979	3/28/1985	F	3/28/1985	18	N/A	N/A	E	2	Decreasing	3/20/2008	N/A
Cactus, Chisos Mountain hedgehog (Echinocereus chisoensis var. chisoensis)	2	9/30/1988	12/8/1993	F	12/8/1993	40	791,900	16	T	9	Stable	N/A	N/A

*Earlier drafts and final plans for some individual species may have become incorporated into later multi-species or ecosystem plans.

www.fws.gov/endangered

GENERAL SPECIES INFORMATION					RECOVERY PLAN INFORMATION						SPECIES/RECOVERY STATUS		
Species Name	Lead Region	Date Listed	Date of First Final Plan	Plan Status*	Date of Current or Active Plan	Number of Actions Implemented	Estimated Costs for Recovery	Estimated Time to Recovery (years)	Listing Classification	Recovery Priority Number	FY 2008 Species' Status	Date 5-Year Status Review Initiated	Date 5-Year Status Review Completed
Cactus, Cochise pincushion (Coryphantha robbinsorum)	2	1/9/1986	9/27/1993	F	9/27/1993	23	276,000	10	T	8	Unknown	4/21/2006	3/20/2007
Cactus, Key tree (Pilosocereus robinii)	4	7/19/1984	5/18/1999	F	5/18/1999	1404	N/A	N/A	E	5C	Decreasing	N/A	N/A
Cactus, Knowlton (Pediocactus knowltonii)	2	11/28/1979	3/29/1985	F	3/29/1985	15	N/A	N/A	E	2	Stable	4/23/2007	N/A
Cactus, Kuenzler hedgehog (Echinocereus fendleri var. kuenzleri)	2	11/28/1979	3/28/1985	F	3/28/1985	15	N/A	N/A	E	12C	Stable	4/1/2004	6/7/2005
Cactus, Lee pincushion (Coryphantha sneedii var. leei)	2	11/26/1979	3/21/1986	F	3/21/1986	20	N/A	N/A	T	3	Stable	N/A	N/A
Cactus, Lloyd's Mariposa (Echinomastus mariposensis)	2	12/6/1979	4/13/1990	F	4/13/1990	27	N/A	N/A	T	2	Stable	N/A	N/A
Cactus, Mesa Verde (Sclerocactus mesae-verdae)	2	11/29/1979	3/30/1984	F	3/30/1984	12	N/A	N/A	T	8C	Decreasing	2/2/2005	N/A
Cactus, Nellie cory (Coryphantha minima)	2	12/8/1979	9/20/1984	F	9/20/1984	10	N/A	N/A	E	2	Unknown	N/A	N/A
Cactus, Nichol's Turk's head (Echinocactus horizon halonius var. nicholii)	2	11/28/1979	4/14/1986	F	4/14/1986	19	N/A	N/A	E	3	Stable	4/23/2007	N/A
Cactus, Peebles Navajo (Pediocactus peeblesianus peeblesianus)	2	11/28/1979	3/30/1984	F	3/30/1984	18	N/A	N/A	E	6	Unknown	4/21/2006	8/28/2008
Cactus, Pima pineapple (Coryphantha scheeri var. robustispina)	2	9/23/1993	N/A	N/A	N/A	N/A	N/A	N/A	E	3	Unknown	2/2/2005	2/8/2007
Cactus, San Rafael (Pediocactus despainii)	6	9/16/1987	N/A	D	10/2/1995	N/A	N/A	N/A	E	11	Decreasing	N/A	N/A
Cactus, Siler pincushion (Pediocactus (=Echinocactus,=Utahia) sileri)	2	11/26/1979	4/14/1986	F	4/14/1986	15	N/A	N/A	T	8	Stable	4/21/2006	N/A
Cactus, Sneed pincushion (Coryphantha sneedii var. sneedii)	2	12/7/1979	3/21/1986	F	3/21/1986	20	N/A	N/A	E	9	Stable	N/A	N/A
Cactus, star (Astrophytum asterias)	2	10/18/1993	11/6/2003	F	11/6/2003	21	N/A	N/A	E	2C	Decreasing	N/A	N/A
Cactus, Tobusch fishhook (Ancistrocactus tobuschii)	2	12/8/1979	3/18/1987	F	3/18/1987	26	N/A	N/A	E	2	Decreasing	3/20/2008	N/A
Cactus, Uinta Basin hookless (Sclerocactus glaucus)	6	11/13/1979	9/27/1990	F	9/27/1990	17	103,000	10	T	8C	Unknown	12/14/2006	3/28/2008
Cactus, Winkler (Pediocactus winkleri)	6	8/20/1998	N/A	D	10/2/1995	N/A	N/A	N/A	T	11C	Decreasing	N/A	N/A
Cactus, Wright fishhook (Sclerocactus wrightiae)	6	10/11/1979	12/24/1985	F	12/24/1985	18	N/A	N/A	E	11	Decreasing	8/3/2005	8/25/2008
Campion, fringed (Silene polypetala)	4	1/18/1991	N/A	D	10/1/1996	21	N/A	N/A	E	8	Unknown	6/21/2005	N/A
Capa rosa (Callicarpa ampla)	4	4/22/1992	7/31/1995	F	7/31/1995	20	N/A	N/A	E	11	Unknown	N/A	N/A
Catchfly, Spalding's (Silene spaldingii)	1	10/10/2001	10/12/2007	F	10/12/2007	71	N/A	N/A	T	8C	Stable	4/29/2008	N/A
Cat's-eye, Terlingua Creek (Cryptantha crassipes)	2	9/30/1991	4/5/1994	F	4/5/1994	39	1,161,750	30	E	5C	Decreasing	3/20/2008	N/A
Ceanothus, coyote (Ceanothus ferrisae)	8	2/3/1995	9/30/1998	F	9/30/1998	180	N/A	N/A	E	14	Unknown	N/A	N/A
Ceanothus, Pine Hill (Ceanothus roderickii)	8	10/18/1996	8/30/2002	F	8/30/2002	52	N/A	N/A	E	5C	Decreasing	N/A	N/A

*Earlier drafts and final plans for some individual species may have become incorporated into later multi-species or ecosystem plans.

www.fws.gov/endangered

Species Name	Lead Region	Date Listed	Date of First Final Plan	Plan Status*	Date of Current or Active Plan	Number of Actions Implemented	Estimated Costs for Recovery	Estimated Time to Recovery (years)	Listing Classification	Recovery Priority Number	FY 2008 Species' Status	Date 5-Year Status Review Initiated	Date 5-Year Status Review Completed
Ceanothus, Vail Lake (Ceanothus ophiochilus)	8	10/13/1998	N/A	N/A	N/A	N/A	N/A	N/A	T	2	Stable	2/14/2007	7/10/2008
Centaury, spring-loving (Centaurium namophilum)	8	5/20/1985	9/28/1990	F	9/28/1990	82	N/A	N/A	T	14	Unknown	7/7/2005	N/A
Chaff-flower, round-leaved (Achyranthes splendens var. rotundata)	1	3/26/1986	N/A	D	10/5/1993	50	N/A	N/A	E	3	Decreasing	3/8/2007	N/A
Chaffseed, American (Schwalbea americana)	5	9/29/1992	9/29/1995	F	9/29/1995	16	N/A	N/A	E	7	Unknown	1/23/2008	N/A
Checker-mallow, Keck's (Sidalcea keckii)	8	2/16/2000	N/A	N/A	N/A	N/A	N/A	N/A	E	8	Unknown	7/7/2005	1/10/2008
Checker-mallow, Kenwood Marsh (Sidalcea oregana ssp. valida)	8	10/22/1997	N/A	N/A	N/A	N/A	N/A	N/A	E	3C	Unknown	3/5/2008	N/A
Checker-mallow, Nelson's (Sidalcea nelsoniana)	1	2/12/1993	9/30/1998	RD(1)	9/22/2008	73	16,490,000	25	T	2	Stable	7/6/2005	N/A
Checker-mallow, pedate (Sidalcea pedata)	8	8/31/1984	7/31/1998	F	7/31/1998	22	N/A	N/A	E	5C	Decreasing	N/A	N/A
Checkermallow, Wenatchee Mountains (Sidalcea oregana var. calva)	1	12/22/1999	9/30/2004	F	9/30/2004	28	896,000	13	E	3	Stable	N/A	N/A
Chumbo, Higo (Harrisia portoricensis)	4	8/8/1990	11/12/1996	F	11/12/1996	18	N/A	N/A	T	14	Stable	9/12/2005	N/A
Chupacallos (Pleodendron macranthum)	4	11/25/1994	9/11/1998	F	9/11/1998	19	N/A	N/A	E	8	Unknown	N/A	N/A
Clarkia, Pismo (Clarkia speciosa ssp. immaculata)	8	12/15/1994	9/28/1998	F	9/28/1998	36	N/A	N/A	E	3C	Decreasing	3/22/2006	N/A
Clarkia, Presidio (Clarkia franciscana)	8	2/3/1995	9/30/1998	F	9/30/1998	180	N/A	N/A	E	5	Decreasing	N/A	N/A
Clarkia, Springville (Clarkia springvillensis)	8	9/14/1998	N/A	N/A	N/A	N/A	N/A	N/A	T	8	Unknown	7/7/2005	N/A
Cliff-rose, Arizona (Purshia (=Cowania) subintegra)	2	5/29/1984	6/16/1995	F	6/16/1995	34	N/A	N/A	E	2	Unknown	4/23/2007	N/A
Clover, Monterey (Trifolium trichocalyx)	8	8/12/1998	12/20/2004	F	6/17/2005	46	N/A	N/A	E	5C	Unknown	N/A	N/A
Clover, running buffalo (Trifolium stoloniferum)	3	6/5/1987	6/8/1989	RF(1)	6/27/2007	18	N/A	N/A	E	8	Decreasing	7/19/2005	N/A
Clover, showy Indian (Trifolium amoenum)	8	10/22/1997	N/A	N/A	N/A	N/A	N/A	N/A	E	2	Decreasing	3/22/2006	1/10/2008
Cobana negra (Stahlia monosperma)	4	4/5/1990	11/1/1996	F	11/1/1996	14	N/A	N/A	T	8	Improving	9/21/2007	N/A
Coneflower, smooth (Echinacea laevigata)	4	10/8/1992	4/18/1995	F	4/18/1995	10	N/A	N/A	E	5	Stable	7/29/2008	N/A
Coneflower, Tennessee purple (Echinacea tennesseensis)	4	7/5/1979	2/14/1983	RF(1)	11/14/1989	23	114,000	4	E	8	Stable	9/21/2007	N/A
Cory cactus, bunched (Coryphantha ramillosa)	2	12/6/1979	4/13/1990	F	4/13/1990	27	N/A	N/A	T	8	Unknown	N/A	N/A
Crownbeard, big-leaved (Verbesina dissita)	8	10/7/1996	N/A	N/A	N/A	N/A	N/A	N/A	T	5C	Decreasing	N/A	N/A
Crownscale, San Jacinto Valley (Atriplex coronata var. notatior)	8	10/13/1998	N/A	N/A	N/A	N/A	N/A	N/A	E	3	Unknown	3/22/2006	3/31/2008

*Earlier drafts and final plans for some individual species may have become incorporated into later multi-species or ecosystem plans.

www.fws.gov/endangered

GENERAL SPECIES INFORMATION			RECOVERY PLAN INFORMATION						SPECIES/RECOVERY STATUS				
Species Name	Lead Region	Date Listed	Date of First Final Plan	Plan Status*	Date of Current or Active Plan	Number of Actions Implemented	Estimated Costs for Recovery	Estimated Time to Recovery (years)	Listing Classification	Recovery Priority Number	FY 2008 Species' Status	Date 5-Year Status Review Initiated	Date 5-Year Status Review Completed
Cycladenia, Jones (Cycladenia jonesii (=humilis))	6	5/5/1986	N/A	N/A	N/A	N/A	N/A	N/A	T	8	Stable	N/A	N/A
Daisy, lakeside (Hymenoxys herbacea)	3	6/23/1988	9/19/1990	F	9/19/1990	17	1,591,600	14	T	8	Stable	4/22/2008	N/A
Daisy, Maguire (Erigeron maguirei)	6	9/5/1985	8/15/1995	F	8/15/1995	11	N/A	N/A	T	14	Stable	4/7/2006	5/19/2008
Daisy, Parish's (Erigeron parishii)	8	8/24/1994	N/A	D	9/30/1997	22	N/A	N/A	T	8C	Unknown	3/5/2008	N/A
Daisy, Willamette (Erigeron decumbens var. decumbens)	1	1/25/2000	N/A	D	9/22/2008	73	16,490,000	25	E	3C	Stable	7/6/2005	N/A
Dawn-flower, Texas prairie (Hymenoxys texana)	2	3/13/1986	4/13/1990	F	4/13/1990	26	N/A	N/A	E	5C	Stable	N/A	N/A
Desert-parsley, Bradshaw's (Lomatium bradshawii)	1	9/30/1988	8/13/1993	RD(1)	9/22/2008	73	16,490,000	25	E	5	Stable	7/6/2005	N/A
Dogweed, ashy (Thymophylla tephroleuca)	2	7/19/1984	7/29/1988	F	7/29/1988	20	N/A	N/A	E	5	Unknown	N/A	N/A
Dropwort, Canby's (Oxypolis canbyi)	4	2/25/1986	4/10/1990	F	4/10/1990	16	N/A	N/A	E	5	Stable	7/28/2006	N/A
Dudleya, Conejo (Dudleya abramsii ssp. parva)	8	1/29/1997	9/30/1999	F	9/30/1999	21	N/A	N/A	T	2C	Stable	3/5/2008	N/A
Dudleya, marcescent (Dudleya cymosa ssp. marcescens)	8	1/29/1997	9/30/1999	F	9/30/1999	21	N/A	N/A	T	9	Unknown	3/5/2008	N/A
Dudleya, Santa Clara Valley (Dudleya setchellii)	8	2/3/1995	9/30/1998	F	9/30/1998	180	N/A	N/A	E	2C	Unknown	N/A	N/A
Dudleya, Santa Cruz Island (Dudleya nesiotica)	8	7/31/1997	9/26/2000	F	9/26/2000	28	51,920,000	40	T	8	Stable	N/A	N/A
Dudleya, Verity's (Dudleya verityi)	8	1/29/1997	9/30/1999	F	9/30/1999	21	N/A	N/A	T	2C	Unknown	3/5/2008	N/A
Dudleyea, Santa Monica Mountains (Dudleya cymosa ssp. ovatifolia)	8	1/29/1997	9/30/1999	F	9/30/1999	21	N/A	N/A	T	UNK	Decreasing	N/A	N/A
Dwarf-flax, Marin (Hesperolinon congestum)	8	2/3/1995	9/30/1998	F	9/30/1998	180	N/A	N/A	T	8C	Unknown	N/A	N/A
Erubia (Solanum drymophilum)	4	8/26/1988	7/9/1992	F	7/9/1992	15	N/A	N/A	E	2C	Unknown	N/A	N/A
Evening-primrose, Antioch Dunes (Oenothera deltoides ssp. howellii)	8	5/27/1978	3/21/1980	RF(1)	4/25/1984	30	N/A	N/A	E	3	Stable	2/14/2007	7/10/2008
Evening-primrose, Eureka Valley (Oenothera avita ssp. eurekensis)	8	5/27/1978	12/13/1982	F	12/13/1982	42	N/A	N/A	E	15	Stable	7/7/2005	9/24/2007
Evening-primrose, San Benito (Camissonia benitensis)	8	2/12/1985	9/19/2006	F	9/21/2006	32	2,438,000	50	T	5	Stable	2/14/2007	N/A
Fiddleneck, large-flowered (Amsinckia grandiflora)	8	5/8/1985	9/29/1997	F	9/29/1997	28	N/A	N/A	E	5	Decreasing	3/5/2008	N/A
Flannelbush, Mexican (Fremontodendron mexicanum)	8	10/13/1998	N/A	N/A	N/A	N/A	N/A	N/A	E	2	Improving	2/14/2007	N/A
Flannelbush, Pine Hill (Fremontodendron californicum ssp. decumbens)	8	10/18/1996	8/30/2002	F	8/30/2002	52	N/A	N/A	E	6C	Decreasing	N/A	N/A
Fleabane, Zuni (Erigeron rhizomatus)	2	4/26/1985	9/30/1988	F	9/30/1988	11	N/A	N/A	T	8	Stable	2/2/2005	9/27/2007
Four-o'clock, MacFarlane's (Mirabilis macfarlanei)	1	11/29/1979	3/27/1985	RF(1)	6/30/2000	25	N/A	N/A	T	2	Stable	4/11/2006	N/A
Frankenia, Johnston's (Frankenia johnstonii)	2	8/7/1984	5/24/1988	F	5/24/1988	N/A	N/A	N/A	E	14	Stable	N/A	N/A

*Earlier drafts and final plans for some individual species may have become incorporated into later multi-species or ecosystem plans.

www.fws.gov/endangered

Recovery Data as of September 30, 2008

GENERAL SPECIES INFORMATION					RECOVERY PLAN INFORMATION				SPECIES/RECOVERY STATUS				
Species Name	Lead Region	Date Listed	Date of First Final Plan	Plan Status*	Date of Current or Active Plan	Number of Actions Implemented	Estimated Costs for Recovery	Estimated Time to Recovery (years)	Listing Classification	Recovery Priority Number	FY 2008 Species' Status	Date 5-Year Status Review Initiated	Date 5-Year Status Review Completed
Fringepod, Santa Cruz Island (Thysanocarpus conchuliferus)	8	7/31/1997	9/26/2000	F	9/26/2000	28	51,920,000	40	E	8	Stable	2/14/2007	N/A
Fringe-tree, pygmy (Chionanthus pygmaeus)	4	1/21/1987	5/18/1999	F	5/18/1999	1404	N/A	N/A	E	2	Unknown	N/A	N/A
Fritillary, Gentner's (Fritillaria gentneri)	1	12/10/1999	8/28/2003	F	8/28/2003	24	3,126,000	16	E	2	Decreasing	4/29/2008	N/A
Gardenia (=Na'u), Hawaiian (Gardenia brighamii)	1	8/21/1985	9/30/1993	F	9/30/1993	147	N/A	N/A	E	2	Stable	4/11/2006	1/18/2008
Geranium, Hawaiian red-flowered (Geranium arboreum)	1	5/13/1992	7/29/1997	F	7/29/1997	41	N/A	N/A	E	2	Decreasing	N/A	N/A
Gerardia, sandplain (Agalinis acuta)	5	9/7/1988	9/20/1989	F	9/20/1989	24	N/A	N/A	E	5C	Stable	1/16/2008	N/A
Gilia, Hoffmann's slender-flowered (Gilia tenuiflora ssp. hoffmannii)	8	7/31/1997	9/26/2000	F	9/26/2000	28	51,920,000	40	E	8	Stable	N/A	N/A
Gilia, Monterey (Gilia tenuiflora ssp. arenaria)	8	6/22/1992	9/29/1998	F	9/29/1998	44	N/A	N/A	E	9	Stable	3/22/2006	3/31/2008
Goetzea, beautiful (Goetzea elegans)	4	4/19/1985	4/28/1987	F	4/28/1987	23	N/A	N/A	E	8	Improving	9/27/2006	N/A
Goldenrod, Blue Ridge (Solidago spithamaea)	4	3/28/1985	10/28/1987	F	10/28/1987	17	N/A	N/A	T	8	Unknown	7/29/2008	N/A
Goldenrod, Houghton's (Solidago houghtonii)	3	7/18/1988	9/17/1997	F	9/17/1997	28	506,500	11	T	8C	Stable	10/4/2007	N/A
Goldenrod, Short's (Solidago shortii)	4	9/5/1985	5/25/1988	F	5/25/1988	19	N/A	N/A	E	8	Stable	7/26/2005	10/25/2007
Goldenrod, white-haired (Solidago albopilosa)	4	4/7/1988	9/28/1993	F	9/28/1993	25	305,300	10	T	8	Stable	7/26/2005	N/A
Goldfields, Burke's (Lasthenia burkei)	8	12/2/1991	N/A	N/A	N/A	N/A	N/A	N/A	E	2C	Unknown	2/14/2007	9/30/2008
Goldfields, Contra Costa (Lasthenia conjugens)	8	6/18/1997	3/7/2006	F	12/15/2005	192	N/A	N/A	E	5C	Unknown	2/14/2007	9/30/2008
Gooseberry, Miccosukee (Ribes echinellum)	4	7/18/1985	N/A	E	N/A	N/A	N/A	N/A	T	11	Stable	4/26/2007	7/15/2008
Gourd, Okeechobee (Cucurbita okeechobeensis ssp. okeechobeensis)	4	7/12/1993	5/18/1999	F	5/18/1999	1404	N/A	N/A	E	3	Decreasing	4/16/2008	N/A
Grass, Colusa (Neostapfia colusana)	8	3/26/1997	3/7/2006	F	12/15/2005	192	N/A	N/A	T	2C	Stable	3/22/2006	7/10/2008
Grass, Eureka Dune (Swallenia alexandrae)	8	5/27/1978	12/13/1982	F	12/13/1982	42	N/A	N/A	E	13	Stable	7/7/2005	9/24/2007
Grass, Solano (Tuctoria mucronata)	8	9/29/1978	9/11/1985	F	12/15/2005	192	N/A	N/A	E	2	Stable	2/14/2007	N/A
Grass, Tennessee yellow-eyed (Xyris tennesseensis)	4	7/26/1991	6/24/1994	F	6/24/1994	16	N/A	N/A	E	8	Stable	N/A	N/A
Ground-plum, Guthrie's (=Pyne's) (Astragalus bibullatus)	4	9/26/1991	N/A	N/A	N/A	N/A	N/A	N/A	E	2	Stable	7/29/2008	N/A
Groundsel, San Francisco Peaks (Senecio franciscanus)	2	11/22/1983	7/21/1987	F	7/21/1987	9	N/A	N/A	T	8	Unknown	4/23/2007	N/A
Gumplant, Ash Meadows (Grindelia fraxino-pratensis)	8	5/20/1985	9/28/1990	F	9/28/1990	82	N/A	N/A	T	14	Unknown	7/7/2005	1/10/2008
Ha'iwale (Cyrtandra crenata)	1	3/28/1994	8/10/1998	F	8/10/1998	28	N/A	N/A	E	5	Decreasing	N/A	N/A
Ha'iwale (Cyrtandra dentata)	1	10/10/1996	8/10/1998	F	8/10/1998	28	N/A	N/A	E	8	Stable	7/6/2005	8/2/2007
Ha'iwale (Cyrtandra giffardii)	1	3/4/1994	9/26/1996	F	9/26/1996	78	9,395,000	20	E	2	Decreasing	N/A	N/A
Ha'iwale (Cyrtandra limahuliensis)	1	2/25/1994	9/20/1995	F	9/20/1995	89	N/A	N/A	T	14	Decreasing	4/29/2008	N/A

*Earlier drafts and final plans for some individual species may have become incorporated into later multi-species or ecosystem plans.

www.fws.gov/endangered

Species Name	Lead Region	Date Listed	Date of First Final Plan	Plan Status*	Date of Current or Active Plan	Number of Actions Implemented	Estimated Costs for Recovery	Estimated Time to Recovery (years)	Listing Classification	Recovery Priority Number	FY 2008 Species' Status	Date 5-Year Status Review Initiated	Date 5-Year Status Review Completed
Ha'iwale (Cyrtandra munroi)	1	5/15/1992	9/29/1995	F	9/29/1995	107	N/A	N/A	E	5	Decreasing	N/A	N/A
Ha'iwale (Cyrtandra polyantha)	1	3/28/1994	8/10/1998	F	8/10/1998	28	N/A	N/A	E	5	Improving	3/8/2007	N/A
Ha'iwale (Cyrtandra subumbellata)	1	10/10/1996	8/10/1998	F	8/10/1998	28	N/A	N/A	E	8	Improving	4/11/2006	1/18/2008
Ha'iwale (Cyrtandra tintinnabula)	1	3/4/1994	9/26/1996	F	9/26/1996	78	9,395,000	20	E	5	Improving	N/A	N/A
Ha'iwale (Cyrtandra viridiflora)	1	10/10/1996	8/10/1998	F	8/10/1998	28	N/A	N/A	E	5	Decreasing	3/8/2007	N/A
Haha (Cyanea acuminata)	1	10/10/1996	8/10/1998	F	8/10/1998	28	N/A	N/A	E	11	Stable	3/8/2007	N/A
Haha (Cyanea asarifolia)	1	2/25/1994	9/20/1995	F	9/20/1995	89	N/A	N/A	E	5	Decreasing	3/8/2007	N/A
Haha (Cyanea copelandii ssp. copelandii)	1	3/4/1994	9/26/1996	F	9/26/1996	78	9,395,000	20	E	6	Decreasing	N/A	N/A
Haha (Cyanea copelandii ssp. haleakalaensis)	1	9/3/1999	9/19/2002	F	7/10/1999	56	33,900,000	11	E	6	Decreasing	N/A	N/A
Haha (Cyanea dunbarii)	1	10/10/1996	5/20/1998	F	5/20/1998	29	N/A	N/A	E	5	Stable	4/11/2006	1/18/2008
Haha (Cyanea glabra)	1	9/3/1999	9/19/2002	F	7/10/1999	56	33,900,000	11	E	5	Decreasing	N/A	N/A
Haha (Cyanea grimesiana ssp. grimesiana)	1	10/10/1996	7/10/1999	F	7/10/1999	56	33,900,000	11	E	6	Stable	N/A	N/A
Haha (Cyanea grimesiana ssp. obatae)	1	6/27/1994	8/10/1998	F	8/10/1998	28	N/A	N/A	E	6	Improving	7/6/2005	8/2/2007
Haha (Cyanea hamatiflora ssp. carlsonii)	1	3/4/1994	9/26/1996	F	9/26/1996	78	9,395,000	20	E	6	Stable	3/8/2007	N/A
Haha (Cyanea hamatiflora ssp. hamatiflora)	1	9/3/1999	9/19/2002	F	7/10/1999	56	33,900,000	11	E	6	Improving	3/8/2007	N/A
Haha (Cyanea humboldtiana)	1	10/10/1996	8/10/1998	F	8/10/1998	28	N/A	N/A	E	5	Decreasing	4/29/2008	N/A
Haha (Cyanea koolauensis)	1	10/10/1996	8/10/1998	F	8/10/1998	28	N/A	N/A	E	5	Decreasing	4/29/2008	N/A
Haha (Cyanea lobata)	1	5/15/1992	7/29/1997	F	7/29/1997	41	N/A	N/A	E	2	Stable	N/A	N/A
Haha (Cyanea longiflora)	1	10/10/1996	8/10/1998	F	8/10/1998	28	N/A	N/A	E	11	Decreasing	3/8/2007	N/A
Haha (Cyanea macrostegia ssp. gibsonii)	1	9/20/1991	9/29/1995	F	9/29/1995	107	N/A	N/A	E	6	Stable	4/11/2006	1/18/2008
Haha (Cyanea mannii)	1	10/8/1992	9/26/1996	F	9/26/1996	29	24,784,000	21	E	2	Decreasing	N/A	N/A
Haha (Cyanea mceldowneyi)	1	5/15/1992	7/29/1997	F	7/29/1997	41	N/A	N/A	E	2	Stable	4/11/2006	1/18/2008
Haha (Cyanea pinnatifida)	1	10/29/1991	8/10/1998	F	8/10/1998	28	N/A	N/A	E	5	Stable	7/6/2005	8/2/2007
Haha (Cyanea platyphylla)	1	10/10/1996	5/11/1998	F	9/26/1996	78	9,395,000	20	E	5	Decreasing	4/11/2006	N/A
Haha (Cyanea procera)	1	10/8/1992	9/26/1996	F	9/26/1996	29	24,784,000	21	E	5	Stable	4/11/2006	1/18/2008
Haha (Cyanea recta)	1	10/10/1996	8/23/1998	F	9/20/1995	89	N/A	N/A	T	2	Decreasing	4/29/2008	N/A
Haha (Cyanea remyi)	1	10/10/1996	8/23/1998	F	9/20/1995	89	N/A	N/A	E	2	Decreasing	4/29/2008	N/A
Haha (Cyanea shipmanii)	1	3/4/1994	9/26/1996	F	9/26/1996	78	9,395,000	20	E	2	Stable	3/8/2007	N/A
Haha (Cyanea st.-johnii)	1	10/10/1996	8/10/1998	F	8/10/1998	28	N/A	N/A	E	5	Improving	7/6/2005	8/2/2007
Haha (Cyanea stictophylla)	1	3/4/1994	9/26/1996	F	9/26/1996	78	9,395,000	20	E	2	Stable	N/A	N/A
Haha (Cyanea superba)	1	9/11/1991	8/10/1998	F	8/10/1998	28	N/A	N/A	E	5	Decreasing	7/6/2005	8/2/2007
Haha (Cyanea truncata)	1	3/28/1994	8/10/1998	F	8/10/1998	28	N/A	N/A	E	5	Stable	7/6/2005	8/2/2007
Haha (Cyanea undulata)	1	9/20/1991	5/31/1994	F	5/31/1994	60	N/A	N/A	E	11	Decreasing	4/11/2006	1/18/2008
Hala pepe (Pleomele hawaiiensis)	1	10/10/1996	5/11/1998	F	9/26/1996	78	9,395,000	20	E	2	Stable	N/A	N/A
Harebells, Avon Park (Crotalaria avonensis)	4	4/27/1993	5/18/1999	F	5/18/1999	1404	N/A	N/A	E	5C	Decreasing	9/27/2006	7/13/2007
Harperella (Ptilimnium nodosum)	5	9/28/1988	3/5/1991	F	3/5/1991	25	N/A	N/A	E	8	Decreasing	1/16/2008	N/A
Hau kuahiwi (Hibiscadelphus giffardianus)	1	10/10/1996	5/11/1998	F	9/26/1996	78	9,395,000	20	E	5	Stable	4/11/2006	1/18/2008

*Earlier drafts and final plans for some individual species may have become incorporated into later multi-species or ecosystem plans.

www.fws.gov/endangered

Species Name	GENERAL SPECIES INFORMATION Lead Region	Date Listed	RECOVERY PLAN INFORMATION Date of First Final Plan	Plan Status*	Date of Current or Active Plan	Number of Actions Implemented	Estimated Costs for Recovery	Estimated Time to Recovery (years)	Listing Classification	Recovery Priority Number	SPECIES/RECOVERY STATUS FY 2008 Species' Status	Date 5-Year Status Review Initiated	Date 5-Year Status Review Completed
Hau kuahiwi (Hibiscadelphus hualalaiensis)	1	10/10/1996	5/11/1998	F	9/26/1996	78	9,395,000	20	E	5	Stable	4/11/2006	1/18/2008
Hau kuahiwi (Hibiscadelphus woodii)	1	10/10/1996	8/23/1998	F	9/20/1995	89	N/A	N/A	E	5	Decreasing	7/6/2005	8/2/2007
Heartleaf, dwarf-flowered (Hexastylis naniflora)	4	4/14/1989	N/A	N/A	N/A	N/A	N/A	N/A	T	14	Unknown	9/20/2005	N/A
Heather, mountain golden (Hudsonia montana)	4	10/20/1980	9/14/1983	F	9/14/1983	17	N/A	N/A	T	8C	Unknown	7/28/2006	N/A
Heau (Exocarpos luteolus)	1	2/25/1994	9/20/1995	F	9/20/1995	89	N/A	N/A	E	5	Decreasing	4/29/2008	N/A
Hedyotis, Na Pali beach (Hedyotis st-johnii)	1	9/30/1991	9/20/1995	F	9/20/1995	89	N/A	N/A	E	8	Decreasing	3/8/2007	N/A
Hibiscus, Clay's (Hibiscus clayi)	1	2/25/1994	9/20/1995	F	9/20/1995	89	N/A	N/A	E	5	Stable	4/11/2006	1/18/2008
Higuero de sierra (Crescentia portoricensis)	4	12/4/1987	9/23/1991	F	9/23/1991	20	N/A	N/A	E	14	Improving	9/21/2007	N/A
Holei (Ochrosia kilaueaensis)	1	3/4/1994	9/26/1996	F	9/26/1996	78	9,395,000	20	E	5	Capivity	N/A	N/A
Holly, Cook's (Ilex cookii)	4	6/16/1987	1/31/1991	F	1/31/1991	19	N/A	N/A	E	5	Unknown	N/A	N/A
Honohono (Haplostachys haplostachya)	1	11/29/1979	N/A	D	9/20/1993	37	N/A	N/A	E	2	Improving	N/A	N/A
Howellia, water (Howellia aquatilis)	6	7/14/1994	N/A	D	9/24/1996	40	N/A	N/A	T	7	Improving	4/18/2007	N/A
Hypericum, highlands scrub (Hypericum cumulicola)	4	1/21/1987	5/18/1999	F	5/18/1999	1404	N/A	N/A	E	2	Unknown	4/26/2007	9/5/2008
Iagu, Hayun (=(Guam), Tronkon guafi (Rota)) (Serianthes nelsonii)	1	2/18/1987	2/2/1994	F	2/2/1994	61	N/A	N/A	E	2	Decreasing	N/A	N/A
Iliau, dwarf (Wilkesia hobdyi)	1	6/22/1992	9/20/1995	F	9/20/1995	89	N/A	N/A	E	2	Stable	4/29/2008	N/A
Indian paintbrush, San Clemente Island (Castilleja grisea)	8	9/12/1977	1/26/1984	F	1/26/1984	54	N/A	N/A	E	14	Stable	7/1/2005	9/24/2007
Ipomopsis, Holy Ghost (Ipomopsis sancti-spiritus)	2	3/23/1994	9/26/2002	F	9/26/2002	29	6,375,000	20	E	5C	Stable	7/21/2004	N/A
Iris, dwarf lake (Iris lacustris)	3	9/28/1988	N/A	N/A	N/A	N/A	N/A	N/A	T	8C	Stable	10/4/2007	N/A
Irisette, white (Sisyrinchium dichotomum)	4	9/26/1991	4/10/1995	F	4/10/1995	16	N/A	N/A	E	8	Unknown	N/A	N/A
Ischaemum, Hilo (Ischaemum byrone)	1	3/4/1994	9/26/1996	F	9/26/1996	78	9,395,000	20	E	5	Decreasing	4/29/2008	N/A
Ivesia, Ash Meadows (Ivesia kingii var. eremica)	8	5/20/1985	9/28/1990	F	9/28/1990	82	N/A	N/A	T	8	Unknown	N/A	N/A
Jacquemontia, beach (Jacquemontia reclinata)	4	11/24/1993	5/18/1999	F	5/18/1999	1404	N/A	N/A	E	2	Decreasing	6/21/2005	5/30/2007
Jewelflower, California (Caulanthus californicus)	8	7/19/1990	9/30/1998	F	9/30/1998	223	N/A	N/A	E	2	Decreasing	3/22/2006	N/A
Jewelflower, Metcalf Canyon (Streptanthus albidus ssp. albidus)	8	2/3/1995	9/30/1998	F	9/30/1998	180	N/A	N/A	E	3C	Unknown	N/A	N/A
Jewelflower, Tiburon (Streptanthus niger)	8	2/3/1995	9/30/1998	F	9/30/1998	180	N/A	N/A	E	5C	Unknown	N/A	N/A
Joint-vetch, sensitive (Aeschynomene virginica)	5	5/20/1992	9/29/1995	F	9/29/1995	25	662,000	20	T	2	Unknown	12/16/2008	N/A
Kamakahala (Labordia cyrtandrae)	1	10/10/1996	8/10/1998	F	8/10/1998	28	N/A	N/A	E	5	Decreasing	4/11/2006	1/18/2008
Kamakahala (Labordia lydgatei)	1	9/20/1991	5/31/1994	F	5/31/1994	60	N/A	N/A	E	11	Decreasing	3/8/2007	N/A
Kamakahala (Labordia tinifolia var. lanaiensis)	1	9/3/1999	9/19/2002	F	7/10/1999	56	33,900,000	11	E	6	Decreasing	N/A	N/A

*Earlier drafts and final plans for some individual species may
have become incorporated into later multi-species or ecosystem plans.

www.fws.gov/endangered

	GENERAL SPECIES INFORMATION		RECOVERY PLAN INFORMATION						SPECIES/RECOVERY STATUS				
Species Name	Lead Region	Date Listed	Date of First Final Plan	Plan Status*	Date of Current or Active Plan	Number of Actions Implemented	Estimated Costs for Recovery	Estimated Time to Recovery (years)	Listing Classification	Recovery Priority Number	FY 2008 Species' Status	Date 5-Year Status Review Initiated	Date 5-Year Status Review Completed
Kamakahala (Labordia tinifolia var. wahiawaensis)	1	10/10/1996	8/23/1998	F	9/20/1995	89	N/A	N/A	E	6	Decreasing	3/8/2007	N/A
Kamakahala (Labordia triflora)	1	9/3/1999	9/19/2002	F	7/10/1999	56	33,900,000	11	E	5	Stable	4/11/2006	1/18/2008
Kamanomano (Cenchrus agrimonioides)	1	10/10/1996	7/10/1999	F	7/10/1999	56	33,900,000	11	E	5	Improving	3/8/2007	N/A
Kauai hau kuahiwi (Hibiscadelphus distans)	1	4/29/1986	6/5/1996	F	6/5/1996	23	2,713,000	20	E	2	Improving	3/8/2007	N/A
Kaulu (Colubrina oppositifolia)	1	3/4/1994	9/26/1996	F	9/26/1996	78	9,395,000	20	E	5	Decreasing	N/A	N/A
Kaulu (Pteralyxia kauaiensis)	1	2/25/1994	9/20/1995	F	9/20/1995	89	9,395,000	N/A	E	8	Decreasing	4/29/2008	N/A
Kio'ele (Hedyotis coriacea)	1	5/15/1992	7/29/1997	F	7/29/1997	41	N/A	N/A	E	2	Decreasing	4/11/2006	1/18/2008
Kiponapona (Phyllostegia racemosa)	1	10/10/1996	5/11/1998	F	9/26/1996	78	9,395,000	20	E	2	Decreasing	N/A	N/A
Ko'oko'olau (Bidens micran ha ssp. kalealaha)	1	5/15/1992	7/29/1997	F	7/29/1997	41	N/A	N/A	E	9	Decreasing	N/A	N/A
Ko'oko'olau (Bidens wiebkei)	1	10/8/1992	9/26/1996	F	9/26/1996	29	24,784,000	21	E	2	Decreasing	N/A	N/A
Ko'oloa'ula (Abutilon menziesii)	1	9/26/1986	9/29/1995	F	9/29/1995	107	N/A	N/A	E	2	Decreasing	N/A	N/A
Kohe malama malama o kanaloa (Kanaloa kahoolawensis)	1	9/3/1999	9/19/2002	F	7/10/1999	56	33,900,000	11	E	1	Decreasing	4/11/2006	1/18/2008
Koki'o (Kokia drynarioides)	1	12/4/1984	5/6/1994	F	5/6/1994	104	N/A	N/A	E	2	Stable	3/8/2007	N/A
Koki'o (Kokia kauaiensis)	1	10/10/1996	8/23/1998	F	9/20/1995	89	N/A	N/A	E	5	Stable	4/29/2008	N/A
Koki'o ke'oke'o (Hibiscus arnottianus ssp. immaculatus)	1	10/8/1992	9/26/1996	F	9/26/1996	29	24,784,000	21	E	3	Decreasing	N/A	N/A
Koki'o ke'oke'o (Hibiscus waimeae ssp. hannerae)	1	10/10/1996	8/23/1998	F	9/20/1995	89	N/A	N/A	E	3	Stable	4/29/2008	N/A
Koki'o, Cooke's (Kokia cookei)	1	11/29/1979	5/27/1998	F	5/27/1998	36	6,365,000	30	E	5	Captivity	4/11/2006	1/18/2008
Kolea (Myrsine juddii)	1	10/10/1996	8/10/1998	F	8/10/1998	28	N/A	N/A	E	8	Decreasing	4/11/2006	1/18/2008
Kolea (Myrsine linearifolia)	1	10/10/1996	8/23/1998	F	9/20/1995	89	N/A	N/A	T	2	Decreasing	N/A	N/A
Kopa (Hedyotis schlechtendahliana var. remyi)	1	9/3/1999	9/19/2002	F	7/10/1999	56	33,900,000	11	E	6	Captivity	4/11/2006	1/18/2008
Kuahiwi laukahi (Plantago hawaiensis)	1	3/4/1994	9/26/1996	F	9/26/1996	78	9,395,000	20	E	5	Decreasing	N/A	N/A
Kuahiwi laukahi (Plantago princeps)	1	11/10/1994	7/10/1999	F	7/10/1999	56	33,900,000	11	E	5	Stable	4/29/2008	N/A
Kuawawaenohu (Aisinidendron lychnoides)	1	10/10/1996	8/23/1998	F	9/20/1995	89	N/A	N/A	E	2	Decreasing	4/29/2008	N/A
Kula wahine noho (Isodendrion pyrifolium)	1	3/4/1994	9/26/1996	F	9/26/1996	78	9,395,000	20	E	2	Decreasing	4/11/2006	1/18/2008
Kulu'i (Nototrichium humile)	1	10/29/1991	8/10/1998	F	8/10/1998	28	N/A	N/A	E	8	Stable	4/11/2006	1/18/2008
Ladies'-tresses, Canelo Hills (Spiranthes delitescens)	2	1/6/1997	N/A	N/A	N/A	N/A	N/A	N/A	E	2C	Stable	N/A	N/A
Ladies'-tresses, Navasota (Spiranthes parksii)	2	5/6/1982	9/21/1984	F	9/21/1984	12	N/A	N/A	E	2	Decreasing	9/21/2007	N/A
Ladies'-tresses, Ute (Spiranthes diluvialis)	6	1/17/1992	N/A	D	9/21/1995	N/A	N/A	N/A	T	14C	Improving	10/12/2004	N/A
Larkspur, Baker's (Delphinium baker)	8	1/26/2000	N/A	N/A	N/A	N/A	N/A	N/A	E	5	Stable	N/A	N/A
Larkspur, San Clemente Island (Delphinium variegatum ssp. kinkiense)	8	9/12/1977	1/26/1984	F	1/26/1984	54	N/A	N/A	E	9	Stable	7/7/2005	3/31/2008
Larkspur, yellow (Delphinium luteum)	8	1/26/2000	N/A	N/A	N/A	N/A	N/A	N/A	E	8C	Unknown	N/A	N/A
Lau 'ehu (Panicum niihauense)	1	10/10/1996	7/10/1999	F	7/10/1999	56	33,900,000	11	E	2	Stable	4/11/2006	1/18/2008

*Earlier drafts and final plans for some individual species may have become incorporated into later multi-species or ecosystem plans.

www.fws.gov/endangered

Species Name	Lead Region	Date Listed	Date of First Final Plan	Plan Status*	Date of Current or Active Plan	Number of Actions Implemented	Estimated Costs for Recovery	Estimated Time to Recovery (years)	Listing Classification	Recovery Priority Number	FY 2008 Species' Status	Date 5-Year Status Review Initiated	Date 5-Year Status Review Completed
Laulihilihi (Schiedea stellarioides)	1	10/10/1996	8/23/1998	F	9/20/1995	89	N/A	N/A	E	2	Decreasing	4/29/2008	N/A
Layia, beach (Layia carnosa)	8	6/22/1992	9/29/1998	F	9/29/1998	44	N/A	N/A	E	8	Unknown	2/14/2007	N/A
Lead-plant, Crenulate (Amorpha crenulata)	4	7/18/1985	5/18/1999	F	5/18/1999	1404	N/A	N/A	E	5C	Decreasing	9/27/2006	9/21/2007
Leather flower, Alabama (Clematis socialis)	4	9/26/1986	12/27/1989	F	12/27/1989	19	N/A	N/A	E	5	Decreasing	6/14/2005	N/A
Leather flower, Morefield's (Clematis morefieldii)	4	5/20/1992	5/3/1994	F	5/3/1994	14	N/A	N/A	E	8	Stable	6/14/2005	N/A
Lessingia, San Francisco (Lessingia germanorum (=L.g. var. germanorum))	8	6/19/1997	10/6/2003	F	10/6/2003	76	N/A	N/A	E	2C	Decreasing	N/A	N/A
Liliwai (Acaena exigua)	1	5/15/1992	7/29/1997	F	7/29/1997	41	N/A	N/A	E	5	Decreasing	4/11/2006	N/A
Lily, Minnesota dwarf trout (Erythronium propullans)	3	3/26/1986	12/16/1987	F	12/16/1987	11	N/A	N/A	E	5C	Decreasing	4/22/2008	N/A
Lily, Pitkin Marsh (Lilium pardalinum ssp. pitkinense)	8	10/22/1997	N/A	N/A	N/A	N/A	N/A	N/A	E	5C	Stable	3/5/2008	N/A
Lily, Western (Lilium occidentale)	8	8/17/1994	3/31/1998	F	3/31/1998	23	N/A	N/A	E	2	Decreasing	3/5/2008	N/A
Liveforever, Laguna Beach (Dudleya stolonifera)	8	10/13/1998	N/A	N/A	N/A	N/A	N/A	N/A	T	8	Unknown	N/A	N/A
Liveforever, Santa Barbara Island (Dudleya traskiae)	8	5/27/1978	6/27/1985	F	6/27/1985	16	N/A	N/A	E	8	Unknown	7/7/2005	1/10/2008
Lo'ulu (Pritchardia affinis)	1	3/4/1994	9/26/1996	F	9/26/1996	78	9,395,000	20	E	5	Stable	4/11/2006	1/18/2008
Lo'ulu (Pritchardia kaalae)	1	10/10/1996	8/10/1998	F	8/10/1998	28	N/A	N/A	E	5	Stable	N/A	N/A
Lo'ulu (Pritchardia munroi)	1	10/8/1992	9/26/1996	F	9/26/1996	29	24,784,000	21	E	5	Stable	4/29/2008	N/A
Lo'ulu (Pritchardia napaliensis)	1	10/10/1996	8/23/1998	F	9/20/1995	89	N/A	N/A	E	5	Decreasing	4/29/2008	N/A
Lo'ulu (Pritchardia remota)	1	8/21/1996	3/31/1998	F	3/31/1998	33	N/A	N/A	E	2	Stable	3/8/2007	N/A
Lo'ulu (Pritchardia schattaueri)	1	10/10/1996	5/11/1998	F	9/26/1996	78	9,395,000	20	E	5	Stable	3/8/2007	N/A
Lo'ulu (Pritchardia viscosa)	1	10/10/1996	8/23/1998	F	9/20/1995	89	N/A	N/A	E	5	Decreasing	4/11/2006	1/18/2008
Locoweed, Fassett's (Oxytropis campestris var. chartacea)	3	9/28/1988	3/29/1991	F	3/29/1991	6	425,000	14	T	9	Stable	7/27/2007	N/A
Lomatium, Cook's (Lomatium cookii)	1	11/7/2002	N/A	D	9/22/2006	53	N/A	N/A	E	2C	Decreasing	N/A	N/A
Loosestrife, rough-leaved (Lysimachia asperulaefolia)	4	6/12/1987	4/19/1995	F	4/19/1995	15	N/A	N/A	E	8	Stable	7/29/2008	N/A
Lousewort, Furbish (Pedicularis furbishiae)	5	5/27/1978	6/29/1983	RF(1)	7/2/1991	21	149,000	7	E	14	Decreasing	8/10/2005	4/7/2007
Love grass, Fosberg's (Eragrostis fosbergii)	1	10/10/1996	8/10/1998	F	8/10/1998	28	N/A	N/A	E	5	Decreasing	N/A	N/A
Lupine, clover (Lupinus tidestromii)	8	6/22/1992	9/29/1998	F	9/29/1998	44	N/A	N/A	E	5	Decreasing	3/5/2008	N/A
Lupine, Kincaid's (Lupinus sulphureus (=oreganus) ssp. kincaidii (=var. kincaidii))	1	1/25/2000	N/A	D	9/22/2008	73	16,490,000	25	T	6C	Unknown	7/6/2005	N/A
Lupine, Nipomo Mesa (Lupinus nipomensis)	8	3/20/2000	N/A	N/A	N/A	N/A	N/A	N/A	E	5	Decreasing	N/A	N/A
Lupine, scrub (Lupinus aridorum)	4	4/7/1987	1/29/1990	RF(1)	6/20/1996	35	N/A	N/A	E	2C	Decreasing	4/26/2007	11/27/2007
Ma'o hau hele (=native yellow hibiscus) (Hibiscus brackenridgei)	1	11/10/1994	7/10/1999	F	7/10/1999	56	33,900,000	11	E	2	Decreasing	3/8/2007	N/A
Ma'oli'oli (Schiedea apokremnos)	1	9/30/1991	9/20/1995	F	9/20/1995	89	N/A	N/A	E	8	Decreasing	4/29/2008	N/A

*Earlier drafts and final plans for some individual species may have become incorporated into later multi-species or ecosystem plans.

Species Name	Lead Region	Date Listed	Date of First Final Plan	Plan Status*	Date of Current or Active Plan	Number of Actions Implemented	Estimated Costs for Recovery	Estimated Time to Recovery (years)	Listing Classification	Recovery Priority Number	FY 2008 Species' Status	Date 5-Year Status Review Initiated	Date 5-Year Status Review Completed
Ma oli oli (Schiedea kealiae)	1	10/10/1996	8/10/1998	F	8/10/1998	28	N/A	N/A	E	8	Decreasing	4/29/2008	N/A
Mahoe (Alectryon macrococcus)	1	5/15/1992	7/29/1997	F	7/29/1997	41	N/A	N/A	E	5	Decreasing	4/29/2008	N/A
Makou (Peucedanum sandwicense)	1	2/25/1994	9/20/1995	F	9/20/1995	89	N/A	N/A	T	8	Decreasing	N/A	N/A
Malacothrix, island (Malacothrix squalida)	8	7/31/1997	9/26/2000	F	9/26/2000	28	51,920,000	40	E	5	Decreasing	N/A	N/A
Malacothrix, Santa Cruz Island (Malacothrix indecora)	8	7/31/1997	9/26/2000	F	9/26/2000	28	51,920,000	40	E	2	Unknown	N/A	N/A
Mallow, Kern (Eremalche kernensis)	8	7/19/1990	9/30/1998	F	9/30/1998	223	N/A	N/A	E	2	Unknown	3/22/2006	N/A
Mallow, Peter's Mountain (Iliamna corei)	5	5/12/1986	9/28/1990	F	9/28/1990	12	153,000	10	E	8	Stable	1/16/2008	9/30/2008
Manaca, palma de (Calyptronoma rivalis)	4	2/6/1990	6/25/1992	F	6/25/1992	18	N/A	N/A	T	8	Improving	9/21/2007	N/A
Manioc, Walker's (Manihot walkerae)	2	10/2/1991	12/12/1993	F	12/12/1993	27	N/A	N/A	E	5	Decreasing	3/23/2007	N/A
Manzanita, Del Mar (Arctostaphylos glandulosa ssp. crassifolia)	8	10/7/1996	N/A	N/A	N/A	N/A	N/A	N/A	E	6C	Decreasing	N/A	N/A
Manzanita, Ione (Arctostaphylos myrtifolia)	8	5/26/1999	N/A	N/A	N/A	N/A	N/A	N/A	T	5C	Decreasing	3/5/2008	N/A
Manzanita, Morro (Arctostaphylos morroensis)	8	12/15/1994	9/28/1998	F	9/28/1998	36	N/A	N/A	T	8	Stable	3/22/2006	3/31/2008
Manzanita, pallid (Arctostaphylos pallida)	8	4/22/1998	N/A	D	4/7/2003	211	N/A	N/A	T	11C	Decreasing	N/A	N/A
Manzanita, Presidio (Arctostaphylos hookeri var. ravenii)	8	11/29/1979	10/6/2003	F	10/6/2003	76	N/A	N/A	E	12	Stable	N/A	N/A
Manzanita, Santa Rosa Island (Arctostaphylos confertiflora)	8	7/31/1997	9/26/2000	F	9/26/2000	28	51,920,000	40	E	2	Stable	3/22/2006	1/10/2008
Mapele (Cyrtandra cyaneoides)	1	10/10/1996	8/23/1998	F	9/20/1995	89	N/A	N/A	E	2	Decreasing	4/29/2008	N/A
Mariposa lily, Tiburon (Calochortus tiburonensis)	8	2/3/1995	9/30/1998	F	9/30/1998	180	N/A	N/A	T	17	Stable	3/5/2008	N/A
Meadowfoam, Butte County (Limnanthes floccosa ssp. californica)	8	6/8/1992	3/7/2006	F	12/15/2005	192	N/A	N/A	E	3C	Unknown	3/22/2006	7/10/2008
Meadowfoam, large-flowered woolly (Limnanthes floccosa ssp. grandiflora)	1	11/7/2002	N/A	D	9/22/2006	53	N/A	N/A	E	3C	Improving	N/A	N/A
Meadowfoam, Sebastopol (Limnanthes vinculans)	8	12/2/1991	N/A	N/A	N/A	N/A	N/A	N/A	E	2C	Unknown	2/14/2007	9/30/2008
Meadowrue, Cooley's (Thalictrum cooleyi)	4	2/7/1989	4/21/1994	F	4/21/1994	16	N/A	N/A	E	2	Stable	4/26/2007	N/A
Mehamehame (Flueggea neowawraea)	1	11/10/1994	7/10/1999	F	7/10/1999	56	33,900,000	11	E	5	Decreasing	3/8/2007	N/A
Mesa-mint, Otay (Pogogyne nudiuscula)	8	8/3/1993	9/3/1998	F	9/3/1998	14	N/A	N/A	E	2C	Unknown	N/A	N/A
Mesa-mint, San Diego (Pogogyne abramsii)	8	10/29/1978	9/3/1998	F	9/3/1998	14	N/A	N/A	E	5	Unknown	N/A	N/A
Milkpea, Small's (Galactia smallii)	4	7/18/1985	5/18/1999	F	5/18/1999	1404	N/A	N/A	E	5C	Decreasing	6/21/2005	N/A
Milk-vetch, Applegate's (Astragalus applegatei)	8	7/28/1993	4/10/1998	F	4/10/1998	26	N/A	N/A	E	5	Improving	8/15/2007	N/A
Milk-vetch, Ash meadows (Astragalus phoenix)	8	5/20/1985	9/28/1990	F	9/28/1990	82	N/A	N/A	T	8	Stable	3/5/2008	N/A
Milk-vetch, Braunton's (Astragalus brauntonii)	8	1/29/1997	9/30/1999	F	9/30/1999	21	N/A	N/A	E	8	Stable	2/14/2007	N/A

*Earlier drafts and final plans for some individual species may have become incorporated into later multi-species or ecosystem plans.

www.fws.gov/endangered

Species Name	GENERAL SPECIES INFORMATION – Lead Region	Date Listed	RECOVERY PLAN INFORMATION – Date of First Final Plan	Plan Status*	Date of Current or Active Plan	Number of Actions Implemented	Estimated Costs for Recovery	Estimated Time to Recovery (years)	SPECIES/RECOVERY STATUS – Listing Classification	Recovery Priority Number	FY 2008 Species' Status	Date 5-Year Status Review Initiated	Date 5-Year Status Review Completed
Milk-vetch, Clara Hunt's (Astragalus clarianus)	8	10/22/1997	N/A	N/A	N/A	N/A	N/A	N/A	E	5C	Unknown	3/5/2008	N/A
Milk-vetch, Coachella Valley (Astragalus lentiginosus var. coachellae)	8	10/6/1998	N/A	N/A	N/A	N/A	N/A	N/A	E	6C	Decreasing	3/22/2006	N/A
Milk-vetch, coastal dunes (Astragalus tener var. titi)	8	8/12/1998	12/20/2004	F	6/17/2005	46	N/A	N/A	E	6C	Stable	3/5/2008	N/A
Milk-vetch, Cushenbury (Astragalus albens)	8	8/24/1994	N/A	D	9/30/1997	22	N/A	N/A	E	2C	Unknown	N/A	N/A
Milk-vetch, Deseret (Astragalus desereticus)	6	10/20/1999	N/A	N/A	N/A	N/A	N/A	N/A	T	14	Improving	4/18/2007	N/A
Milk-vetch, Fish Slough (Astragalus lentiginosus var. piscinensis)	8	10/6/1998	9/30/1998	F	9/30/1998	100	N/A	N/A	T	9C	Unknown	6/4/2007	N/A
Milk-vetch, heliotrope (Astragalus montii)	6	11/6/1987	N/A	D	9/27/1995	N/A	N/A	N/A	T	8	Stable	N/A	N/A
Milk-vetch, Holmgren (Astragalus holmgreniorum)	6	9/28/2001	9/22/2006	F	9/29/2006	52	18,839,000	30	E	5C	Decreasing	4/7/2006	4/13/2007
Milk-vetch, Jesup's (Astragalus robbinsii var. jesupi)	5	6/5/1987	11/21/1989	F	11/21/1989	17	N/A	N/A	E	6	Stable	1/16/2008	N/A
Milk-vetch, Lane Mountain (Astragalus jaegerianus)	8	10/6/1998	N/A	N/A	N/A	N/A	N/A	N/A	E	8	Stable	3/22/2006	7/10/2008
Milk-vetch, Mancos (Astragalus humillimus)	2	6/27/1985	12/20/1989	F	12/20/1989	13	N/A	N/A	E	5C	Stable	4/23/2007	N/A
Milk-vetch, Osterhout (Astragalus osterhoutii)	6	7/13/1989	9/30/1992	F	9/30/1992	13	N/A	N/A	E	2	Stable	N/A	N/A
Milk-vetch, Peirson's (Astragalus magdalenae var. peirsonii)	8	10/6/1998	N/A	N/A	N/A	N/A	N/A	N/A	T	9	Stable	7/21/2008	9/30/2008
Milk-vetch, Sentry (Astragalus cremnophylax var. cremnophylax)	2	12/5/1990	9/28/2006	F	9/28/2006	45	N/A	N/A	E	6	Improving	4/23/2007	N/A
Milk-vetch, Shivwits (Astragalus ampullarioides)	6	9/28/2001	9/22/2006	F	9/29/2006	52	18,839,000	30	E	5	Decreasing	4/7/2006	4/13/2007
Milk-vetch, triple-ribbed (Astragalus tricarinatus)	8	10/6/1998	N/A	N/A	N/A	N/A	N/A	N/A	E	2	Stable	3/5/2008	N/A
Milk-vetch, Ventura Marsh (Astragalus pyonostachyus var. lanosissimus)	8	5/21/2001	N/A	N/A	N/A	N/A	N/A	N/A	E	6C	Decreasing	N/A	N/A
Milkweed, Mead's (Asclepias meadii)	3	9/1/1988	9/22/2003	F	9/22/2003	43	5,930,000	30	T	8C	Stable	N/A	N/A
Milkweed, Welsh's (Asclepias welshii)	6	10/28/1987	9/30/1992	F	9/30/1992	16	250,000	18	T	11C	Unknown	N/A	N/A
Mint, Garrett's (Dicerandra christmanii)	4	11/1/1985	5/18/1999	F	5/18/1999	1404	N/A	N/A	E	2C	Unknown	4/16/2008	9/30/2008
Mint, Lakela's (Dicerandra immaculata)	4	5/15/1985	5/18/1999	F	5/18/1999	1404	N/A	N/A	E	2C	Decreasing	4/26/2007	9/30/2008
Mint, longspurred (Dicerandra cornutissima)	4	11/1/1985	7/1/1987	F	7/1/1987	26	N/A	N/A	E	2C	Decreasing	4/26/2007	9/11/2008
Mint, scrub (Dicerandra frutescens)	4	11/1/1985	5/18/1999	F	5/18/1999	1404	N/A	N/A	E	2	Unknown	4/16/2008	N/A
Monardella, willowy (Monardella linoides ssp. viminea)	8	10/13/1998	N/A	N/A	N/A	N/A	N/A	N/A	E	6	Decreasing	3/22/2006	4/8/2008
Monkey-flower, Michigan (Mimulus glabratus var. michiganensis)	3	6/21/1990	9/17/1997	F	9/17/1997	17	N/A	N/A	E	9C	Stable	N/A	N/A

*Earlier drafts and final plans for some individual species may have become incorporated into later multi-species or ecosystem plans.

www.fws.gov/endangered

GENERAL SPECIES INFORMATION					RECOVERY PLAN INFORMATION				SPECIES/RECOVERY STATUS				
Species Name	Lead Region	Date Listed	Date of First Final Plan	Plan Status*	Date of Current or Active Plan	Number of Actions Implemented	Estimated Costs for Recovery	Estimated Time to Recovery (years)	Listing Classifi-cation	Recovery Priority Number	FY 2008 Species' Status	Date 5-Year Status Review Initiated	Date 5-Year Status Review Completed
Monkshood, northern wild (Aconitum noveboracense)	3	5/27/1978	9/23/1983	F	9/23/1983	43	N/A	N/A	T	8	Unknown	4/22/2008	N/A
Morning-glory, Stebbins' (Calystegia stebbinsii)	8	10/18/1996	8/30/2002	F	8/30/2002	52	N/A	N/A	E	5C	Decreasing	N/A	N/A
Mountain balm, Indian Knob (Eriodictyon altissimum)	8	12/15/1994	9/28/1998	F	9/28/1998	36	N/A	N/A	E	8	Stable	3/22/2006	N/A
Mountain-mahogany, Catalina Island (Cercocarpus traskiae)	8	8/8/1997	N/A	N/A	N/A	N/A	N/A	N/A	E	8	Stable	3/22/2006	9/24/2007
Mustard, Carter's (Warea carteri)	4	1/21/1987	5/18/1999	F	5/18/1999	1404	N/A	N/A	E	2	Unknown	4/26/2007	9/30/2008
Mustard, Penland alpine fen (Eutrema penlandii)	6	7/28/1993	N/A	N/A	N/A	N/A	N/A	N/A	T	11C	Stable	N/A	N/A
Mustard, slender-petaled (Thelypodium stenopetalum)	8	8/31/1984	7/31/1998	F	7/31/1998	22	N/A	N/A	E	5C	Unknown	N/A	N/A
Na'ena'e (Dubautia herbstobatae)	1	10/29/1991	8/10/1998	F	8/10/1998	28	N/A	N/A	E	8	Stable	4/11/2006	1/23/2008
Na'ena'e (Dubautia latifolia)	1	5/13/1992	9/20/1995	F	9/20/1995	89	N/A	N/A	E	5	Decreasing	4/29/2008	N/A
Na'ena'e (Dubautia pauciflorula)	1	9/20/1991	5/31/1994	F	5/31/1994	60	N/A	N/A	E	8	Decreasing	3/8/2007	N/A
Na'ena'e (Dubautia plantaginea ssp. humilis)	1	9/3/1999	9/19/2002	F	7/10/1999	56	33,900,000	11	E	8	Decreasing	3/8/2007	N/A
Nani wai'ale'ale (Viola kauaiensis var. wahiawaensis)	1	10/10/1996	8/23/1998	F	9/20/1995	89	N/A	N/A	E	6	Decreasing	3/8/2007	N/A
Nanu (Gardenia mannii)	1	10/10/1996	8/10/1998	F	8/10/1998	28	N/A	N/A	E	5	Stable	4/11/2006	1/18/2008
Naupaka, dwarf (Scaevola coriacea)	1	5/16/1986	7/29/1997	F	7/29/1997	41	N/A	N/A	E	2	Stable	4/29/2008	N/A
Navarretia, few-flowered (Navarretia leucocephala ssp. pauciflora (=N. pauciflora))	8	6/18/1997	3/7/2006	F	12/15/2005	192	N/A	N/A	E	3	Unknown	2/14/2007	7/10/2008
Navarretia, many-flowered (Navarretia leucocephala ssp. plieantha)	8	6/18/1997	3/7/2006	F	12/15/2005	192	N/A	N/A	E	3	Unknown	2/14/2007	N/A
Navarretia, spreading (Navarretia fossalis)	8	10/13/1998	9/3/1998	F	9/3/1998	14	N/A	N/A	T	2	Decreasing	3/22/2006	N/A
Nehe (Lipochaeta fauriei)	1	2/25/1994	9/20/1995	F	9/20/1995	89	N/A	N/A	E	5	Decreasing	4/29/2008	N/A
Nehe (Lipochaeta kamolensis)	1	5/15/1992	7/29/1997	F	7/29/1997	41	N/A	N/A	E	2	Decreasing	3/8/2007	N/A
Nehe (Lipochaeta lobata var. leptophylla)	1	10/29/1991	8/10/1998	F	8/10/1998	28	N/A	N/A	E	3	Decreasing	N/A	N/A
Nehe (Lipochaeta micrantha)	1	2/25/1994	9/20/1995	F	9/20/1995	89	N/A	N/A	E	8	Decreasing	N/A	N/A
Nehe (Lipochaeta tenuifolia)	1	10/29/1991	8/10/1998	F	8/10/1998	28	N/A	N/A	E	8	Stable	N/A	N/A
Nehe (Lipochaeta waimeaensis)	1	2/25/1994	9/20/1995	F	9/20/1995	89	N/A	N/A	E	2	Decreasing	4/29/2008	N/A
Nioi (Eugenia koolauensis)	1	3/28/1994	8/10/1998	F	8/10/1998	28	N/A	N/A	E	5	Decreasing	4/11/2006	1/18/2008
Niterwort, Amargosa (Nitrophila mohavensis)	8	5/20/1985	9/28/1990	F	9/28/1990	82	N/A	N/A	E	8	Unknown	7/7/2005	1/10/2008
No common name (Abutilon eremitopetalum)	1	9/20/1991	9/29/1995	F	9/29/1995	107	N/A	N/A	E	2	Stable	4/29/2008	N/A
No common name (Abutilon sandwicense)	1	10/29/1991	8/10/1998	F	8/10/1998	28	N/A	N/A	E	8	Decreasing	N/A	N/A
No common name (Achyranthes mutica)	1	10/10/1996	7/10/1999	F	7/10/1999	56	33,900,000	11	E	2	Stable	3/8/2007	N/A
No common name (Alsinidendron obovatum)	1	10/29/1991	8/10/1998	F	8/10/1998	28	N/A	N/A	E	5	Improving	7/6/2005	8/2/2007
No common name (Alsinidendron trinerve)	1	10/29/1991	8/10/1998	F	8/10/1998	28	N/A	N/A	E	5	Improving	3/8/2007	N/A

*Earlier drafts and final plans for some individual species may have become incorporated into later multi-species or ecosystem plans.

www.fws.gov/endangered

GENERAL SPECIES INFORMATION					RECOVERY PLAN INFORMATION						SPECIES/RECOVERY STATUS		
Species Name	Lead Region	Date Listed	Date of First Final Plan	Plan Status*	Date of Current or Active Plan	Number of Actions Implemented	Estimated Costs for Recovery	Estimated Time to Recovery (years)	Listing Classification	Recovery Priority Number	FY 2008 Species' Status	Date 5-Year Status Review Initiated	Date 5-Year Status Review Completed
No common name (Alsinidendron viscosum)	1	10/10/1996	8/23/1998	F	9/20/1995	89	N/A	N/A	E	2	Decreasing	3/8/2007	N/A
No common name (Amaranthus brownii)	1	8/21/1996	3/31/1998	F	3/31/1998	33	N/A	N/A	E	5	Unknown	7/6/2005	8/2/2007
No common name (Aristida chaseae)	4	4/27/1993	7/31/1995	F	7/31/1995	22	N/A	N/A	E	11C	Stable	9/21/2007	N/A
No common name (Auerodendron pauciflorum)	4	3/2/1994	9/29/1997	F	9/29/1997	19	N/A	N/A	E	5	Unknown	N/A	N/A
No common name (Bonamia menziesii)	1	11/10/1994	7/10/1999	F	7/10/1999	56	33,900,000	11	E	5	Decreasing	4/29/2008	N/A
No common name (Calyptranthes thomasiana)	4	2/18/1994	9/30/1997	F	9/30/1997	19	N/A	N/A	E	11	Unknown	N/A	N/A
No common name (Catesbaea melanocarpa)	4	3/17/1999	8/18/2005	F	8/18/2005	29	521,000	10	E	5	Stable	9/27/2006	N/A
No common name (Chamaecrista glandulosa var. mirabilis)	4	4/5/1990	5/12/1994	F	5/12/1994	19	N/A	N/A	E	5	Unknown	N/A	N/A
No common name (Chamaesyce halemanui)	1	5/13/1992	9/20/1995	F	9/20/1995	89	N/A	N/A	E	5	Decreasing	4/29/2008	N/A
No common name (Cordia bellonis)	4	1/10/1997	10/1/1999	F	10/1/1999	20	N/A	N/A	E	5	Stable	9/27/2006	N/A
No common name (Cranichis ricartii)	4	11/29/1991	7/15/1996	F	7/15/1996	16	N/A	N/A	E	11	Unknown	9/21/2007	N/A
No common name (Cyanea (=Rollandia) crispa)	1	3/28/1994	8/10/1998	F	8/10/1998	28	N/A	N/A	E	5	Decreasing	3/8/2007	N/A
No common name (Daphnopsis hellerana)	4	6/23/1988	8/7/1992	F	8/7/1992	19	N/A	N/A	E	5	Stable	N/A	N/A
No common name (Delissea rhytidosperma)	1	2/25/1994	9/20/1995	F	9/20/1995	89	N/A	N/A	E	5	Stable	4/11/2006	1/18/2008
No common name (Delissea undulata)	1	10/10/1996	9/26/1996	F	9/26/1996	78	9,395,000	20	E	5	Stable	9/21/2007	N/A
No common name (Eugenia woodburyana)	4	9/9/1994	10/6/1998	F	10/6/1998	21	N/A	N/A	E	8	Improving	9/21/2007	N/A
No common name (Gahnia lanaiensis)	1	9/20/1991	9/29/1995	F	9/29/1995	107	N/A	N/A	E	5	Decreasing	N/A	N/A
No common name (Geocarpon minimum)	4	6/16/1987	7/26/1993	F	7/26/1993	10	N/A	N/A	T	13	Unknown	7/26/2005	N/A
No common name (Gesneria pauciflora)	4	3/7/1995	10/6/1998	F	10/6/1998	19	N/A	N/A	T	11	Stable	N/A	N/A
No common name (Gouania hillebrandii)	1	11/9/1984	7/16/1990	F	7/16/1990	36	306,000	15	E	8	Decreasing	4/29/2008	N/A
No common name (Gouania meyenii)	1	10/29/1991	8/10/1998	F	8/10/1998	28	N/A	N/A	E	8	Decreasing	4/29/2008	N/A
No common name (Gouania vitifolia)	1	6/27/1994	8/10/1998	F	8/10/1998	28	N/A	N/A	E	5	Stable	7/6/2005	8/2/2007
No common name (Hedyotis degeneri)	1	10/29/1991	8/10/1998	F	8/10/1998	28	N/A	N/A	E	5	Decreasing	7/6/2005	8/2/2007
No common name (Hedyotis parvula)	1	10/29/1991	8/10/1998	F	8/10/1998	28	N/A	N/A	E	5	Stable	4/11/2006	1/18/2008
No common name (Hesperomannia arborescens)	1	3/28/1994	8/10/1998	F	8/10/1998	28	N/A	N/A	E	5	Decreasing	3/8/2007	N/A
No common name (Hesperomannia arbuscula)	1	10/29/1991	8/10/1998	F	8/10/1998	28	N/A	N/A	E	5	Decreasing	3/8/2007	N/A
No common name (Hesperomannia lydgatei)	1	9/20/1991	5/31/1994	F	5/31/1994	60	N/A	N/A	E	11	Decreasing	4/29/2008	N/A
No common name (Ilex sintenisii)	4	4/22/1992	7/31/1995	F	7/31/1995	20	N/A	N/A	E	11	Unknown	N/A	N/A
No common name (Lepanthes eltoroensis)	4	11/29/1991	7/15/1996	F	7/15/1996	16	N/A	N/A	E	5	Stable	9/27/2006	N/A
No common name (Leptocereus grantianus)	4	2/26/1993	7/26/1995	F	7/26/1995	19	N/A	N/A	E	5C	Improving	N/A	N/A

*Earlier drafts and final plans for some individual species may have become incorporated into later multi-species or ecosystem plans.

www.fws.gov/endangered

	GENERAL SPECIES INFORMATION			RECOVERY PLAN INFORMATION						SPECIES/RECOVERY STATUS				
Species Name	Lead Region	Date Listed	Date of First Final Plan	Plan Status*	Date of Current or Active Plan	Number of Actions Implemented	Estimated Costs for Recovery	Estimated Time to Recovery (years)	Listing Classification	Recovery Priority Number	FY 2008 Species' Status	Date 5-Year Status Review Initiated	Date 5-Year Status Review Completed
No common name (Lipochaeta venosa)	1	11/29/1979	5/23/1994	F	5/23/1994	38	N/A	N/A	E	5	Stable	N/A	N/A
No common name (Lobelia gaudichaudii ssp. koolauensis)	1	10/10/1996	8/10/1998	F	8/10/1998	28	N/A	N/A	E	6	Decreasing	3/8/2007	N/A
No common name (Lobelia monostachya)	1	10/10/1996	8/10/1998	F	8/10/1998	28	N/A	N/A	E	5	Stable	4/11/2006	1/18/2008
No common name (Lobelia niihauensis)	1	10/29/1991	8/10/1998	F	8/10/1998	28	N/A	N/A	E	8	Decreasing	N/A	N/A
No common name (Lobelia oahuensis)	1	3/28/1994	8/10/1998	F	8/10/1998	28	N/A	N/A	E	5	Decreasing	N/A	N/A
No common name (Lyonia truncata var. proctorii)	4	4/27/1993	7/31/1995	F	7/31/1995	22	N/A	N/A	E	6	Unknown	9/21/2007	N/A
No common name (Lysimachia filifolia)	1	2/25/1994	9/20/1995	F	9/20/1995	89	N/A	N/A	E	2	Stable	3/8/2007	N/A
No common name (Lysimachia lydgatei)	1	5/15/1992	7/29/1997	F	7/29/1997	41	N/A	N/A	E	2	Decreasing	N/A	N/A
No common name (Lysimachia maxima)	1	10/10/1996	5/20/1998	F	5/20/1998	29	N/A	N/A	E	5	Improving	4/11/2006	1/18/2008
No common name (Mariscus fauriei)	1	3/4/1994	9/26/1996	F	9/26/1996	78	9,395,000	20	E	14	Decreasing	N/A	N/A
No common name (Mariscus pennatiformis)	1	11/10/1994	7/10/1999	F	7/10/1999	56	33,900,000	11	E	5	Improving	4/29/2008	N/A
No common name (Mitracarpus maxwelliae)	4	9/9/1994	10/6/1998	F	10/6/1998	21	N/A	N/A	E	5	Stable	9/27/2006	N/A
No common name (Mitracarpus polycladus)	4	9/9/1994	10/6/1998	F	10/6/1998	21	N/A	N/A	E	5	Improving	9/27/2006	N/A
No common name (Munroidendron racemosum)	1	2/25/1994	9/20/1995	F	9/20/1995	89	N/A	N/A	E	5	Stable	4/29/2008	N/A
No common name (Myrcia paganii)	4	2/18/1994	9/29/1997	F	9/29/1997	19	N/A	N/A	E	8	Unknown	N/A	N/A
No common name (Neraudia angulata)	1	10/29/1991	8/10/1998	F	8/10/1998	28	N/A	N/A	E	5	Improving	4/11/2006	1/18/2008
No common name (Neraudia ovata)	1	10/10/1996	5/11/1998	F	9/26/1996	78	9,395,000	20	E	5	Stable	4/11/2006	1/18/2008
No common name (Neraudia sericea)	1	11/10/1994	7/10/1999	F	7/10/1999	56	33,900,000	11	E	5	Decreasing	N/A	N/A
No common name (Nesogenes rotensis)	1	4/8/2004	5/3/2007	F	5/3/2007	45	N/A	N/A	E	2	Decreasing	N/A	N/A
No common name (Osmoxylon mariannense)	1	4/8/2004	5/3/2007	F	5/3/2007	45	N/A	N/A	E	2	Decreasing	N/A	N/A
No common name (Phyllostegia glabra var. lanaiensis)	1	9/20/1991	9/29/1995	F	9/29/1995	107	N/A	N/A	E	6	Decreasing	N/A	N/A
No common name (Phyllostegia hirsuta)	1	10/10/1996	8/10/1998	F	8/10/1998	28	N/A	N/A	E	5	Decreasing	4/11/2006	1/18/2008
No common name (Phyllostegia kaalaensis)	1	10/10/1996	8/10/1998	F	8/10/1998	28	N/A	N/A	E	5	Improving	4/11/2006	1/18/2008
No common name (Phyllostegia knudsenii)	1	10/10/1996	8/23/1998	F	9/20/1995	89	N/A	N/A	E	5	Decreasing	3/8/2007	N/A
No common name (Phyllostegia mannii)	1	10/8/1992	9/26/1996	F	9/26/1996	29	24,784,000	21	E	5	Stable	N/A	N/A
No common name (Phyllostegia mollis)	1	10/29/1991	8/10/1998	F	8/10/1998	28	N/A	N/A	E	5	Decreasing	3/8/2007	N/A
No common name (Phyllostegia parviflora)	1	10/10/1996	7/10/1999	F	7/10/1999	56	33,900,000	11	E	5	Stable	4/11/2006	1/18/2008
No common name (Phyllostegia velutina)	1	10/10/1996	5/11/1998	F	9/26/1996	78	9,395,000	20	E	2	Stable	N/A	N/A
No common name (Phyllostegia waimeae)	1	2/25/1994	9/20/1995	F	9/20/1995	89	N/A	N/A	E	5	Stable	4/11/2006	1/18/2008
No common name (Phyllostegia warshaueri)	1	10/10/1996	5/11/1998	F	9/26/1996	78	9,395,000	20	E	5	Decreasing	N/A	N/A

*Earlier drafts and final plans for some individual species may have become incorporated into later multi-species or ecosystem plans.

www.fws.gov/endangered

31

Recovery Data as of September 30, 2008

Species Name	Lead Region	Date Listed	Date of First Final Plan	Plan Status*	Date of Current or Active Plan	Number of Actions Implemented	Estimated Costs for Recovery	Estimated Time to Recovery (years)	Listing Classification	Recovery Priority Number	FY 2008 Species' Status	Date 5-Year Status Review Initiated	Date 5-Year Status Review Completed
No common name (Phyllostegia wawrana)	1	10/10/1996	8/23/1998	F	9/20/1995	89	N/A	N/A	E	5	Decreasing	3/8/2007	N/A
No common name (Platan hera holochila)	1	10/10/1996	7/10/1999	F	7/10/1999	56	33,900,000	11	E	5	Improving	3/8/2007	N/A
No common name (Poa siphonoglossa)	1	5/13/1992	9/20/1995	F	9/20/1995	89	N/A	N/A	E	5	Stable	4/29/2008	N/A
No common name (Remya kauaiensis)	1	1/14/1991	9/20/1995	F	9/20/1995	89	N/A	N/A	E	5	Decreasing	4/29/2008	N/A
No common name (Remya montgomeryi)	1	1/14/1991	9/20/1995	F	9/20/1995	89	N/A	N/A	E	5	Decreasing	4/29/2008	N/A
No common name (Sanicula mariversa)	1	10/29/1991	8/10/1998	F	8/10/1998	28	N/A	N/A	E	5	Improving	4/11/2006	1/18/2008
No common name (Sanicula purpurea)	1	10/10/1996	7/10/1999	F	7/10/1999	56	33,900,000	11	E	5	Stable	N/A	N/A
No common name (Schiedea haleakalensis)	1	5/15/1992	7/29/1997	F	7/29/1997	41	N/A	N/A	E	2	Decreasing	N/A	N/A
No common name (Schiedea helleri)	1	10/10/1996	8/23/1998	F	9/20/1995	89	N/A	N/A	E	5	Decreasing	4/29/2008	N/A
No common name (Schiedea hookeri)	1	10/10/1996	7/10/1999	F	7/10/1999	56	33,900,000	11	E	8	Decreasing	N/A	N/A
No common name (Schiedea kaalae)	1	10/29/1991	8/10/1998	F	8/10/1998	28	N/A	N/A	E	2	Decreasing	4/11/2006	1/18/2008
No common name (Schiedea kauaiensis)	1	10/10/1996	8/23/1998	F	9/20/1995	89	N/A	N/A	E	5	Stable	4/11/2006	1/18/2008
No common name (Schiedea lydgatei)	1	10/8/1992	9/26/1996	F	9/26/1996	29	24,784,000	21	E	8	Decreasing	N/A	N/A
No common name (Schiedea membranacea)	1	10/10/1996	8/23/1998	F	9/20/1995	89	N/A	N/A	E	2	Decreasing	4/29/2008	N/A
No common name (Schiedea nuttallii)	1	10/10/1996	7/10/1999	F	7/10/1999	56	33,900,000	11	E	5	Decreasing	3/8/2007	N/A
No common name (Schiedea sarmentosa)	1	10/10/1996	5/20/1998	F	5/20/1998	29	N/A	N/A	E	8	Decreasing	N/A	N/A
No common name (Schiedea spergulina var. leiopoda)	1	2/25/1994	9/20/1995	F	9/20/1995	89	N/A	N/A	E	6	Decreasing	4/29/2008	N/A
No common name (Schiedea spergulina var. spergulina)	1	2/25/1994	9/20/1995	F	9/20/1995	89	N/A	N/A	E	9	Decreasing	4/29/2008	N/A
No common name (Schiedea verticillata)	1	8/21/1996	3/31/1998	F	3/31/1998	33	N/A	N/A	E	2	Decreasing	3/8/2007	N/A
No common name (Schoepfia arenaria)	4	4/19/1991	1/10/1992	F	1/10/1992	20	N/A	N/A	T	5C	Unknown	N/A	N/A
No common name (Silene alexandri)	1	10/8/1992	9/26/1996	F	9/26/1996	29	24,784,000	21	E	5	Decreasing	4/11/2006	1/18/2008
No common name (Silene hawaiiensis)	1	3/4/1994	9/26/1996	F	9/26/1996	78	9,395,000	20	T	8	Stable	4/29/2008	N/A
No common name (Silene lanceolata)	1	10/8/1992	9/26/1996	F	9/26/1996	29	24,784,000	21	E	2	Stable	4/29/2008	N/A
No common name (Silene perlmanii)	1	10/29/1991	8/10/1998	F	8/10/1998	28	N/A	N/A	E	5	Decreasing	4/11/2006	1/18/2008
No common name (Spermolepis hawaiiensis)	1	11/10/1994	7/10/1999	F	7/10/1999	56	33,900,000	11	E	5	Stable	4/29/2008	N/A
No common name (Stenogyne angustifolia var. angustifolia)	1	11/29/1979	N/A	D	9/20/1993	37	N/A	N/A	E	2	Decreasing	N/A	N/A
No common name (Stenogyne bifida)	1	10/8/1992	9/26/1996	F	9/26/1996	29	24,784,000	21	E	2	Captivity	4/29/2008	N/A
No common name (Stenogyne campanulata)	1	5/13/1992	9/20/1995	F	9/20/1995	89	N/A	N/A	E	5	Stable	3/8/2007	N/A
No common name (Stenogyne kanehoana)	1	5/13/1992	8/10/1998	F	8/10/1998	28	N/A	N/A	E	5	Stable	4/11/2006	1/18/2008

*Earlier drafts and final plans for some individual species may have become incorporated into later multi-species or ecosystem plans.

www.fws.gov/endangered

Recovery Data as of September 30, 2008

Species Name	Lead Region	Date Listed	Date of First Final Plan	Plan Status*	Date of Current or Active Plan	Number of Actions Implemented	Estimated Costs for Recovery	Estimated Time to Recovery (years)	Listing Classification	Recovery Priority Number	FY 2008 Species' Status	Date 5-Year Status Review Initiated	Date 5-Year Status Review Completed
No common name (Ternstroemia subsessilis)	4	4/22/1992	7/31/1995	F	7/31/1995	20	N/A	N/A	E	5	Unknown	N/A	N/A
No common name (Tetramolopium arenarium)	1	3/4/1994	9/26/1996	F	9/26/1996	78	9,395,000	20	E	5	Stable	N/A	N/A
No common name (Tetramolopium filiforme)	1	10/29/1991	8/10/1998	F	8/10/1998	28	N/A	N/A	E	2	Stable	4/11/2006	1/18/2008
No common name (Tetramolopium lepidotum ssp. lepidotum)	1	10/29/1991	8/10/1998	F	8/10/1998	28	N/A	N/A	E	3	Stable	3/8/2007	N/A
No common name (Tetramolopium remyi)	1	9/20/1991	9/29/1995	F	9/29/1995	107	N/A	N/A	E	2	Decreasing	N/A	N/A
No common name (Tetramolopium rockii)	1	10/8/1992	9/26/1996	F	9/26/1996	29	24,784,000	21	T	14	Stable	N/A	N/A
No common name (Trematolobelia singularis)	1	10/10/1996	8/10/1998	F	8/10/1998	28	N/A	N/A	E	5	Improving	3/8/2007	N/A
No common name (Vernonia proctorii)	4	4/27/1993	7/31/1995	F	7/31/1995	22	N/A	N/A	E	8	Stable	9/21/2007	N/A
No common name (Vigna o-wahuensis)	1	11/10/1994	7/10/1999	F	7/10/1999	56	33,900,000	11	E	5	Decreasing	N/A	N/A
No common name (Viola helenae)	1	9/20/1991	5/31/1994	F	5/31/1994	60	N/A	N/A	E	2	Decreasing	4/11/2006	1/18/2008
No common name (Viola lanaiensis)	1	9/20/1991	9/29/1995	F	9/29/1995	107	N/A	N/A	E	2	Improving	N/A	N/A
No common name (Viola oahuensis)	1	10/10/1996	8/10/1998	F	8/10/1998	28	N/A	N/A	E	5	Decreasing	3/8/2007	N/A
No common name (Xylosma crenatum)	1	5/13/1992	9/20/1995	F	9/20/1995	89	N/A	N/A	E	5	Decreasing	N/A	N/A
Nohoanu (Geranium multiflorum)	1	5/15/1992	7/29/1997	F	7/29/1997	41	N/A	N/A	E	8	Decreasing	N/A	N/A
Oak, Hinckley (Quercus hinckleyi)	2	8/26/1988	9/30/1992	F	9/30/1992	42	605,900	20	T	8	Unknown	3/20/2008	N/A
Oha (Delissea rivularis)	1	10/10/1996	8/23/1998	F	9/20/1995	89	N/A	N/A	E	5	Decreasing	4/29/2008	N/A
Oha (Delissea subcordata)	1	10/10/1996	8/10/1998	F	8/10/1998	28	N/A	N/A	E	5	Improving	4/11/2006	1/18/2008
Ohai (Sesbania tomentosa)	1	11/10/1994	7/10/1999	F	7/10/1999	56	33,900,000	11	E	8	Stable	4/29/2008	N/A
Olulu (Brighamia insignis)	1	2/25/1994	9/20/1995	F	9/20/1995	89	N/A	N/A	E	2	Decreasing	4/11/2006	1/18/2008
Onion, Munz's (Allium munzii)	8	10/13/1998	N/A	N/A	N/A	N/A	N/A	N/A	E	2	Unknown	3/22/2006	N/A
Opuhe (Urera kaalae)	1	10/29/1991	8/10/1998	F	8/10/1998	28	N/A	N/A	E	5	Decreasing	N/A	N/A
Orchid, eastern prairie fringed (Platanthera leucophaea)	3	9/28/1989	9/29/1999	F	9/29/1999	13	5,315,000	20	T	8	Stable	7/27/2007	N/A
Orchid, western prairie fringed (Platanthera praeclara)	3	9/28/1989	9/30/1996	F	9/30/1996	40	2,963,000	10	T	8C	Stable	3/30/2006	N/A
Orcutt grass, California (Orcuttia californica)	8	8/3/1993	9/3/1998	F	9/3/1998	14	N/A	N/A	E	5C	Unknown	N/A	N/A
Orcutt grass, hairy (Orcuttia pilosa)	8	3/26/1997	3/7/2006	F	12/15/2005	192	N/A	N/A	E	2C	Unknown	3/22/2006	N/A
Orcutt grass, Sacramento (Orcuttia viscida)	8	3/26/1997	3/7/2006	F	12/15/2005	192	N/A	N/A	E	5C	Stable	3/22/2006	7/10/2008
Orcutt grass, San Joaquin (Orcuttia inaequalis)	8	3/26/1997	3/7/2006	F	12/15/2005	192	N/A	N/A	T	8	Unknown	2/14/2007	N/A
Orcutt grass, slender (Orcuttia tenuis)	8	3/26/1997	3/7/2006	F	12/15/2005	192	N/A	N/A	T	8	Stable	3/22/2006	N/A
Owl's-clover, fleshy (Castilleja campestris ssp. succulenta)	8	3/26/1997	3/7/2006	F	12/15/2005	192	N/A	N/A	T	9	Decreasing	3/5/2008	N/A
Oxytheca, cushenbury (Oxytheca parishii var. goodmaniana)	8	8/24/1994	N/A	D	9/30/1997	22	N/A	N/A	E	3C	Unknown	N/A	N/A

*Earlier drafts and final plans for some individual species may have become incorporated into later multi-species or ecosystem plans.

www.fws.gov/endangered

33

GENERAL SPECIES INFORMATION						RECOVERY PLAN INFORMATION					SPECIES/RECOVERY STATUS			
Species Name	Lead Region	Date Listed	Date of First Final Plan	Plan Status*	Date of Current or Active Plan	Number of Actions Implemented	Estimated Costs for Recovery	Estimated Time to Recovery (years)	Listing Classifi- cation	Recovery Priority Number	FY 2008 Species' Status	Date 5-Year Status Review Initiated	Date 5-Year Status Review Completed
Paintbrush, ash-grey (Cas tilleja cinerea)	8	9/14/1998	N/A	N/A	N/A	N/A	N/A	N/A	T	8	Unknown	2/14/2007	3/31/2008
Paintbrush, golden (Castilleja levisecta)	1	6/11/1997	8/23/2000	RD(1)	9/22/2008	28	16,490,000	25	T	2	Improving	7/6/2005	9/26/2007
Paintbrush, soft-leaved (Castilleja mollis)	8	7/31/1997	9/26/2000	F	9/26/2000	28	51,920,000	40	E	5	Decreasing	3/22/2006	1/10/2008
Paintbrush, Tiburon (Castilleja affinis ssp. neglecta)	8	2/3/1995	9/30/1998	F	9/30/1998	180	N/A	N/A	E	9C	Unknown	N/A	N/A
Palo colorado (Ternstroemia luquillensis)	4	4/22/1992	7/31/1995	F	7/31/1995	20	N/A	N/A	E	11	Unknown	N/A	N/A
Palo de jazmin (Styrax portoricensis)	4	4/22/1992	7/31/1995	F	7/31/1995	20	N/A	N/A	E	5	Stable	N/A	N/A
Palo de nigua (Cornutia obovata)	4	4/7/1988	8/7/1992	F	8/7/1992	19	N/A	N/A	E	5	Unknown	N/A	N/A
Palo de ramon (Banara vanderbilti)	4	1/14/1987	3/15/1991	F	3/15/1991	19	N/A	N/A	E	5	Unknown	N/A	N/A
Palo de rosa (Ottoschulzia rhodoxylon)	4	4/10/1990	9/20/1994	F	9/20/1994	18	N/A	N/A	E	8	Unknown	9/21/2007	N/A
Pamakani (Tetramolopium capillare)	1	9/30/1994	7/29/1997	F	7/29/1997	41	N/A	N/A	E	2	Decreasing	N/A	N/A
Pamakani (Viola chamissoniana ssp. chamissoniana)	1	10/29/1991	8/10/1998	F	8/10/1998	28	N/A	N/A	E	3	Stable	4/11/2006	1/18/2008
Panicgrass, Carter's (Panicum fauriei var. carteri)	1	10/12/1983	N/A	D	12/9/1993	N/A	515,000	19	E	9	Decreasing	N/A	N/A
Pawpaw, beautiful (Deeringothamnus pulchellus)	4	9/26/1986	5/18/1999	F	5/18/1999	1404	N/A	N/A	E	2	Unknown	4/16/2008	N/A
Pawpaw, four-petal (Asimina tetramera)	4	9/26/1986	5/18/1999	F	5/18/1999	1404	N/A	N/A	E	11	Stable	4/16/2008	N/A
Pawpaw, Rugel's (Deeringothamnus rugelii)	4	9/26/1986	4/5/1988	F	4/5/1988	17	N/A	N/A	E	2	Stable	4/26/2007	9/25/2008
Pelos del diablo (Aristida portoricensis)	4	8/8/1990	5/16/1994	F	5/16/1994	19	N/A	N/A	E	11C	Stable	9/21/2007	N/A
Penny-cress, Kneeland Prairie (Thlaspi californicum)	8	2/9/2000	8/14/2003	F	8/14/2003	15	318,000	10	E	2C	Unknown	7/7/2005	6/20/2006
Pennyroyal, Todsen's (Hedeoma todsenii)	2	1/19/1981	3/22/1985	RF(2)	1/31/2001	17	1,120,300	10	E	8	Stable	4/21/2006	N/A
Penstemon, blowout (Penstemon haydenii)	6	9/1/1987	7/17/1992	F	7/17/1992	29	1,039,000	13	E	11C	Decreasing	N/A	N/A
Pentachaeta, Lyon's (Pentachaeta lyonii)	8	1/29/1997	9/30/1999	F	9/30/1999	21	N/A	N/A	E	2C	Stable	2/14/2007	9/30/2008
Pentachaeta, white-rayed (Pentachaeta bellidiflora)	8	2/3/1995	9/30/1998	F	9/30/1998	180	N/A	N/A	E	8	Stable	N/A	N/A
Peperomia, Wheeler's (Peperomia wheeleri)	4	1/14/1987	11/26/1990	F	11/26/1990	18	N/A	N/A	E	5	Improving	9/27/2006	N/A
Phacelia, clay (Phacelia argillacea)	6	10/29/1978	4/12/1982	F	4/12/1982	14	N/A	N/A	E	2	Decreasing	9/21/2007	N/A
Phacelia, island (Phacelia insularis ssp. insularis)	8	7/31/1997	9/26/2000	F	9/26/2000	28	51,920,000	40	E	6	Decreasing	3/1/2007	7/2/2008
Phacelia, North Park (Phacelia formosula)	6	9/1/1982	3/21/1986	F	3/21/1986	24	N/A	N/A	E	8	Stable	N/A	N/A
Phlox, Texas trailing (Phlox nivalis ssp. texensis)	2	9/30/1991	3/28/1995	F	3/28/1995	48	N/A	N/A	E	3	Stable	N/A	N/A
Phlox, Yreka (Phlox hirsuta)	8	2/3/2000	9/18/2006	F	9/21/2006	19	950,220	10	E	2C	Stable	7/7/2005	9/24/2007
Pigeon wings (Clitoria fragrans)	4	4/27/1993	5/18/1999	F	5/18/1999	1404	N/A	N/A	T	14	Unknown	4/26/2007	9/30/2008
Pilo (Hedyotis mannii)	1	10/8/1992	9/26/1996	F	9/26/1996	29	24,784,000	21	E	5	Decreasing	N/A	N/A

*Earlier drafts and final plans for some individual species may have become incorporated into later multi-species or ecosystem plans.

www.fws.gov/endangered

	GENERAL SPECIES INFORMATION				RECOVERY PLAN INFORMATION					SPECIES/RECOVERY STATUS			
Species Name	Lead Region	Date Listed	Date of First Final Plan	Plan Status*	Date of Current or Active Plan	Number of Actions Implemented	Estimated Costs for Recovery	Estimated Time to Recovery (years)	Listing Classification	Recovery Priority Number	FY 2008 Species' Status	Date 5-Year Status Review Initiated	Date 5-Year Status Review Completed
Pink, swamp (Helonias bullata)	5	9/9/1988	9/30/1991	F	9/30/1991	18	25,500,000	11	T	7C	Unknown	4/21/2006	9/30/2008
Pinkroot gentian (Spigelia gentianoides)	4	11/26/1990	N/A	N/A	N/A	N/A	N/A	N/A	E	2	Stable	4/16/2008	N/A
Piperia, Yadon's (Piperia yadonii)	8	8/12/1998	12/20/2004	F	6/17/2005	46	N/A	N/A	E	2C	Stable	N/A	N/A
Pitaya, Davis' green (Echinocereus viridiflorus var. davisii)	2	12/8/1979	9/20/1984	F	9/20/1984	11	N/A	N/A	E	3	Unknown	N/A	N/A
Pitcher-plant, Alabama canebrake (Sarracenia rubra alabamensis)	4	3/10/1989	10/8/1992	F	10/8/1992	12	N/A	N/A	E	6	Stable	7/29/2008	N/A
Pitcher-plant, green (Sarracenia oreophila)	4	10/21/1979	5/11/1983	RF(2)	12/12/1994	18	N/A	N/A	E	8	Stable	N/A	N/A
Pitcher-plant, mountain sweet (Sarracenia rubra ssp. jonesii)	4	9/30/1988	8/13/1990	F	8/13/1990	16	N/A	N/A	E	3C	Unknown	N/A	N/A
Plum, scrub (Prunus geniculata)	4	1/21/1987	1/29/1987	RF(1)	6/20/1996	35	N/A	N/A	E	2	Decreasing	4/16/2008	N/A
Po'e (Portulaca sclerocarpa)	1	3/4/1994	9/26/1996	F	9/26/1996	78	9,395,000	20	E	2	Stable	N/A	N/A
Pogonia, small whorled (Isotria medeoloides)	5	9/9/1982	1/16/1985	RF(1)	11/13/1992	31	471,500	10	T	14	Stable	1/29/2007	9/30/2008
Polygala, Lewton's (Polygala lewtonii)	4	4/27/1993	5/18/1999	F	5/18/1999	1404	N/A	N/A	E	8	Unknown	N/A	N/A
Polygala, tiny (Polygala smallii)	4	7/18/1985	5/18/1999	F	5/18/1999	1404	N/A	N/A	E	5C	Decreasing	6/21/2005	N/A
Polygonum, Scotts Valley (Polygonum hickmanii)	8	4/8/2003	9/28/1998	F	9/28/1998	30	N/A	N/A	E	5	Unknown	N/A	N/A
Pondberry (Lindera melissifolia)	4	7/31/1986	9/23/1993	F	9/23/1993	30	886,000	10	E	8C	Decreasing	N/A	N/A
Pondweed, Little Aguja (=Creek) (Potamogeton clystocarpus)	2	11/14/1991	6/20/1994	F	6/20/1994	29	N/A	N/A	E	5	Unknown	N/A	N/A
Popcornflower, rough (Plagiobothrys hirtus)	1	1/25/2000	9/25/2003	F	9/25/2003	23	N/A	N/A	E	2C	Stable	4/29/2008	N/A
Popolo ku mai (Solanum incompletum)	1	11/10/1994	7/10/1999	F	7/10/1999	56	33,900,000	11	E	5	Stable	4/11/2006	1/18/2008
Poppy, Sacramento prickly (Argemone pleiacantha ssp. pinnatisecta)	2	8/24/1989	8/31/1994	F	8/31/1994	36	N/A	N/A	E	3	Decreasing	4/21/2006	N/A
Poppy-mallow, Texas (Callirhoe scabriuscula)	2	1/13/1981	3/29/1985	F	3/29/1985	11	N/A	N/A	E	5C	Unknown	N/A	N/A
Potato-bean, Price's (Apios priceana)	4	1/5/1990	2/10/1993	F	2/10/1993	22	491,850	17	T	8	Decreasing	N/A	N/A
Potentilla, Hickman's (Potentilla hickmanii)	8	8/12/1998	12/20/2004	F	6/17/2005	46	N/A	N/A	E	5C	Decreasing	7/29/2008	N/A
Prairie-clover, leafy (Dalea foliosa)	4	5/1/1991	9/30/1996	F	9/30/1996	18	1,905,000	10	E	5	Decreasing	7/29/2008	N/A
Prickly-apple, fragrant (Cereus eriophorus var. fragrans)	4	11/1/1985	5/18/1999	F	5/18/1999	1404	N/A	N/A	E	3	Decreasing	N/A	N/A
Prickly-ash, St Thomas (Zanthoxylum thomasianum)	4	12/20/1985	4/5/1988	F	4/5/1988	25	N/A	N/A	E	5C	Unknown	N/A	N/A
Primrose, Maguire (Primula maguirei)	6	8/21/1985	9/27/1990	F	9/27/1990	8	N/A	N/A	T	5	Stable	N/A	N/A
Pu'uka'a (Cyperus trachysanthos)	1	10/10/1996	7/10/1999	F	7/10/1999	56	33,900,000	11	E	5	Decreasing	4/29/2008	N/A
Pua 'ala (Brighamia rockii)	1	10/8/1992	9/26/1996	F	9/26/1996	29	24,784,000	21	E	2	Stable	4/11/2006	1/18/2008
Pussypaws, Mariposa (Calyptridium pulchellum)	8	9/14/1998	N/A	N/A	N/A	N/A	N/A	N/A	T	8	Unknown	7/7/2005	1/10/2008
Rat leeweed, hairy (Baptisia arachnifera)	4	5/27/1978	3/19/1984	F	3/19/1984	32	N/A	N/A	E	8	Decreasing	7/26/2005	N/A
Reed-mustard, Barneby (Schoenocrambe barnebyi)	6	1/14/1992	9/14/1994	F	9/14/1994	16	N/A	N/A	E	11	Stable	N/A	N/A

*Earlier drafts and final plans for some individual species may have become incorporated into later multi-species or ecosystem plans.

www.fws.gov/endangered

Species Name	Lead Region	Date Listed	Date of First Final Plan	Plan Status*	Date of Current or Active Plan	Number of Actions Implemented	Estimated Costs for Recovery	Estimated Time to Recovery (years)	Listing Classification	Recovery Priority Number	FY 2008 Species' Status	Date 5-Year Status Review Initiated	Date 5-Year Status Review Completed
Reed-mustard, clay (Schoenocrambe argillacea)	6	1/14/1992	9/14/1994	F	9/14/1994	16	N/A	N/A	T	11C	Stable	N/A	N/A
Reed-mustard, shrubby (Schoenocrambe suffrutescens)	6	10/6/1987	9/14/1994	F	9/14/1994	16	N/A	N/A	E	4C	Stable	N/A	N/A
Remya, Maui (Remya mauiensis)	1	1/14/1991	7/29/1997	F	7/29/1997	41	N/A	N/A	E	5	Decreasing	3/8/2007	N/A
Rhododendron, Chapman (Rhododendron chapmanii)	4	5/23/1979	9/8/1983	F	9/8/1983	45	N/A	N/A	E	8C	Stable	N/A	N/A
Ridge-cress, Barneby (Lepidium barnebyanum)	6	9/28/1990	7/23/1993	F	7/23/1993	10	N/A	N/A	E	5C	Unknown	N/A	N/A
Rock-cress, Braun's (Arabis perstellata)	4	1/3/1995	7/22/1997	F	7/22/1997	13	N/A	N/A	E	5	Stable	7/28/2006	N/A
Rock-cress, Hoffmann's (Arabis hoffmannii)	8	7/31/1997	9/26/2000	F	9/26/2000	28	51,920,000	40	E	5	Decreasing	3/22/2006	9/24/2007
Rock-cress, McDonald's (Arabis mcdonaldiana)	8	9/29/1978	2/28/1984	F	2/28/1984	14	N/A	N/A	E	14C	Unknown	N/A	N/A
Rockcress, Santa Cruz Island (Sibara filifolia)	8	8/8/1997	N/A	N/A	N/A	N/A	N/A	N/A	E	2	Stable	7/7/2005	9/11/2006
Rock-cress, shale barren (Arabis serotina)	5	7/13/1989	8/15/1991	F	8/15/1991	15	227,000	11	E	11	Unknown	N/A	N/A
Rosemary, Apalachicola (Conradina glabra)	4	7/12/1993	9/27/1994	F	9/27/1994	9	N/A	N/A	E	8	Stable	4/16/2008	N/A
Rosemary, Cumberland (Conradina verticillata)	4	11/29/1991	7/12/1996	F	7/12/1996	13	325,000	9	T	8	Unknown	N/A	N/A
Rosemary, Etonia (Conradina etonia)	4	7/12/1993	9/27/1994	F	9/27/1994	10	N/A	N/A	E	14	Stable	9/7/2006	6/4/2007
Rosemary, short-leaved (Conradina brevifolia)	4	7/12/1993	5/18/1999	F	5/18/1999	1404	N/A	N/A	E	8C	Unknown	4/26/2007	8/8/2008
Roseroot, Leedy's (Sedum integrifolium ssp. leedyi)	3	4/22/1992	9/25/1998	F	9/25/1998	11	596,000	10	T	9	Stable	4/22/2008	N/A
Rush-pea, slender (Hoffmannseggia tenella)	2	11/1/1985	9/13/1988	F	9/13/1988	15	N/A	N/A	E	2	Stable	4/21/2006	7/11/2008
Rush-rose, island (Helianthemum greenei)	8	7/31/1997	9/26/2000	F	9/26/2000	28	51,920,000	40	T	8	Stable	N/A	N/A
Sandalwood, Lanai (= Iliahi) (Santalum freycinetianum var. lanaiense)	1	1/24/1986	9/29/1995	F	9/29/1995	107	N/A	N/A	E	3	Decreasing	N/A	N/A
Sandlace (Polygonella myriophylla)	4	4/27/1993	5/18/1999	F	5/18/1999	1404	N/A	N/A	E	8	Unknown	N/A	N/A
Sand-verbena, large-fruited (Abronia macrocarpa)	2	9/28/1988	9/30/1992	F	9/30/1992	51	831,900	23	E	2	Stable	4/23/2007	N/A
Sandwort, Bear Valley (Arenaria ursina)	8	9/14/1998	N/A	N/A	N/A	N/A	N/A	N/A	T	8	Unknown	2/14/2007	3/31/2008
Sandwort, Cumberland (Arenaria cumberlandensis)	4	6/23/1988	6/20/1996	F	6/20/1996	18	268,000	9	E	8	Stable	9/21/2007	N/A
Sandwort, Marsh (Arenaria paludicola)	8	8/3/1993	9/28/1998	F	9/28/1998	40	N/A	N/A	E	5	Decreasing	2/14/2007	7/10/2008
Schiedea, Diamond Head (Schiedea adamantis)	1	2/17/1984	2/2/1994	F	2/2/1994	27	N/A	N/A	E	5	Decreasing	4/11/2006	1/18/2008
Seablite, California (Suaeda californica)	8	12/15/1994	N/A	N/A	N/A	N/A	N/A	N/A	E	8	Improving	N/A	N/A
Sedge, golden (Carex lutea)	4	1/23/2002	N/A	N/A	N/A	N/A	N/A	N/A	E	8	Unknown	7/28/2006	N/A
Sedge, Navajo (Carex specuicola)	2	5/8/1985	9/24/1987	F	9/24/1987	12	N/A	N/A	T	8	Decreasing	N/A	N/A
Sedge, white (Carex albida)	8	10/22/1997	N/A	N/A	N/A	N/A	N/A	N/A	E	5C	Decreasing	3/5/2008	N/A

*Earlier drafts and final plans for some individual species may have become incorporated into later multi-species or ecosystem plans.

www.fws.gov/endangered

	GENERAL SPECIES INFORMATION		RECOVERY PLAN INFORMATION							SPECIES/RECOVERY STATUS				
Species Name	Lead Region	Date Listed	Date of First Final Plan	Plan Status*	Date of Current or Active Plan	Number of Actions Implemented	Estimated Costs for Recovery	Estimated Time to Recovery (years)	Listing Classifi-cation	Recovery Priority Number	FY 2008 Species' Status	Date 5-Year Status Review Initiated	Date 5-Year Status Review Completed
Silversword, Mauna Loa (=Ka'u) (Argyroxiphium kauense)	1	4/7/1993	11/21/1995	F	11/21/1995	47	N/A	N/A	E	2	Improving	3/8/2007	N/A
Skullcap, Florida (Scutellaria floridana)	4	5/8/1992	6/22/1994	F	6/22/1994	16	N/A	N/A	T	2	Unknown	4/16/2008	N/A
Skullcap, large-flowered (Scutellaria montana)	4	6/20/1986	5/15/1996	F	5/15/1996	13	N/A	N/A	T	8	Decreasing	9/21/2007	N/A
Snakeroot (Eryngium cuneifolium)	4	1/21/1987	5/18/1999	F	5/18/1999	1404	N/A	N/A	E	2	Unknown	N/A	N/A
Sneezeweed, Virginia (Helenium virginicum)	5	11/3/1998	N/A	D	10/2/2000	N/A	N/A	N/A	T	2	Stable	12/16/2008	N/A
Snowbells, Texas (Styrax texanus)	2	10/12/1984	7/31/1987	F	7/31/1987	31	N/A	N/A	E	3	Stable	4/23/2007	9/12/2008
Spineflower, Ben Lomond (Chorizanthe pungens var. hartwegiana)	8	2/4/1994	9/28/1998	F	9/28/1998	30	N/A	N/A	E	9	Decreasing	3/22/2006	9/24/2007
Spineflower, Howell's (Chorizanthe howellii)	8	6/22/1992	9/29/1998	F	9/29/1998	44	N/A	N/A	E	8	Unknown	3/22/2006	9/24/2007
Spineflower, Monterey (Chorizanthe pungens var. pungens)	8	2/4/1994	9/29/1998	F	9/29/1998	44	N/A	N/A	T	15	Stable	2/14/2007	N/A
Spineflower, Orcutt's (Chorizanthe orcuttiana)	8	10/7/1996	N/A	N/A	N/A	N/A	N/A	N/A	E	5	Unknown	3/22/2006	1/10/2008
Spineflower, Robust (incl. Scotts Valley) (Chorizanthe robusta (incl. vars. robusta and hartwegii)	8	2/4/1994	9/28/1998	F	12/20/2004	21	N/A	N/A	E	3	Unknown	N/A	N/A
Spineflower, slender-horned (Dodecahema leptoceras)	8	9/28/1987	N/A	N/A	N/A	N/A	N/A	N/A	E	1C	Unknown	3/22/2006	N/A
Spineflower, Sonoma (Chorizanthe valida)	8	6/22/1992	9/29/1998	F	9/29/1998	44	N/A	N/A	E	5	Stable	N/A	N/A
Spiraea, Virginia (Spiraea virginiana)	5	6/15/1990	11/13/1992	F	11/13/1992	14	160,700	5	T	8	Stable	N/A	N/A
Spurge, deltoid (Chamaesyce deltoidea ssp. deltoidea)	4	7/18/1985	5/18/1999	F	5/18/1999	1404	N/A	N/A	E	6C	Decreasing	6/21/2005	N/A
Spurge, Garber's (Chamaesyce garberi)	4	7/18/1985	5/18/1999	F	5/18/1999	1404	N/A	N/A	T	8	Stable	9/27/2006	9/6/2007
Spurge, Hoover's (Chamaesyce hooveri)	8	3/26/1997	3/7/2006	F	12/15/2005	192	N/A	N/A	T	8C	Unknown	2/14/2007	N/A
Spurge, telephus (Euphorbia telephioides)	4	5/8/1992	6/22/1994	F	6/22/1994	16	N/A	N/A	T	2C	Stable	4/26/2007	3/6/2008
Stickseed, showy (Hackelia venusta)	1	2/6/2002	12/12/2007	F	12/12/2007	21	N/A	N/A	E	5	Unknown	N/A	N/A
Stonecrop, Lake County (Parvisedum leiocarpum)	8	6/18/1997	3/7/2006	F	12/15/2005	192	N/A	N/A	E	2C	Decreasing	2/14/2007	N/A
Sumac, Michaux's (Rhus michauxii)	4	9/28/1989	4/30/1993	F	4/30/1993	16	N/A	N/A	E	2	Stable	7/29/2008	N/A
Sunburst, Hartweg's golden (Pseudobahia bahiifolia)	8	2/6/1997	N/A	N/A	N/A	N/A	N/A	N/A	E	5C	Unknown	7/7/2005	1/10/2008
Sunburst, San Joaquin adobe (Pseudobahia peirsonii)	8	2/6/1997	N/A	N/A	N/A	N/A	N/A	N/A	T	2	Unknown	7/7/2005	1/10/2008
Sunflower, Pecos (=puzzle, =paradox) (Helianthus paradoxus)	2	10/20/1999	9/15/2005	F	9/15/2005	25	924,000	14	T	8	Improving	4/23/2007	N/A
Sunflower, San Mateo woolly (Eriophyllum latilobum)	8	2/3/1995	9/30/1998	F	9/30/1998	180	N/A	N/A	E	11	Decreasing	N/A	N/A
Sunflower, Schweinitz's (Helian hus schweinitzii)	4	5/7/1991	4/22/1994	F	4/22/1994	11	N/A	N/A	E	5	Unknown	9/20/2005	N/A
Sunray, Ash Meadows (Enceliopsis nudicaulis var. corrugata)	8	5/20/1985	9/28/1990	F	9/28/1990	82	N/A	N/A	T	15	Unknown	N/A	N/A

*Earlier drafts and final plans for some individual species may
have become incorporated into later multi-species or ecosystem plans.

www.fws.gov/endangered

GENERAL SPECIES INFORMATION						RECOVERY PLAN INFORMATION						SPECIES/RECOVERY STATUS		
Species Name	Lead Region	Date Listed	Date of First Final Plan	Plan Status*	Date of Current or Active Plan	Number of Actions Implemented	Estimated Costs for Recovery	Estimated Time to Recovery (years)	Listing Classifi-cation	Recovery Priority Number	FY 2008 Species' Status	Date 5-Year Status Review Initiated	Date 5-Year Status Review Completed
Sunshine, Sonoma (Blennosperma bakeri)	8	12/2/1991	N/A	N/A	N/A	N/A	N/A	N/A	E	5C	Unknown	2/14/2007	9/30/2008
Taraxacum, California (Taraxacum californicum)	8	9/14/1998	N/A	N/A	N/A	N/A	N/A	N/A	E	5	Decreasing	2/14/2007	3/31/2008
Tarplant, Gaviota (Deinandra increscens ssp. villosa)	8	3/20/2000	N/A	N/A	N/A	N/A	N/A	N/A	E	3	Stable	N/A	N/A
Tarplant, Otay (Deinandra (=Hemizonia) conjugens)	8	10/13/1998	12/28/2004	F	12/28/2004	21	N/A	N/A	T	8	Stable	3/22/2006	N/A
Tarplant, Santa Cruz (Holocarpha macradenia)	8	3/20/2000	N/A	N/A	N/A	N/A	N/A	N/A	T	8	Decreasing	N/A	N/A
Thelypody, Howell's spectacular (Thelypodium howellii spectabilis)	1	5/26/1999	6/3/2002	F	6/3/2002	23	768,000	15	T	8	Unknown	3/8/2007	N/A
Thistle, Chorro Creek bog (Cirsium fontinale var. obispoense)	8	12/15/1994	9/28/1998	F	9/28/1998	36	N/A	N/A	E	9	Stable	3/22/2006	9/25/2007
Thistle, fountain (Cirsium fontinale var. fontinale)	8	2/3/1995	9/30/1998	F	9/30/1998	180	N/A	N/A	E	6	Stable	N/A	N/A
Thistle, La Graciosa (Cirsium loncholepis)	8	3/20/2000	N/A	N/A	N/A	N/A	N/A	N/A	E	2	Decreasing	N/A	N/A
Thistle, Loch Lomond coyote (Eryngium constancei)	8	8/1/1985	3/7/2006	F	12/15/2005	192	N/A	N/A	E	8C	Decreasing	2/14/2007	N/A
Thistle, Pitcher's (Cirsium pitcheri)	3	7/18/1988	9/20/2002	F	9/20/2002	27	4,480,000	11	T	8C	Stable	3/30/2006	N/A
Thistle, Sacramento Mountains (Cirsium vinaceum)	2	6/16/1987	9/27/1993	F	9/27/1993	15	N/A	N/A	T	8C	Stable	12/5/2006	N/A
Thistle, Suisun (Cirsium hydrophilum var. hydrophilum)	8	11/20/1997	N/A	N/A	N/A	N/A	N/A	N/A	E	3C	Unknown	2/14/2007	N/A
Thornmint, San Diego (Acanthomintha ilicifolia)	8	10/13/1998	N/A	N/A	N/A	N/A	N/A	N/A	T	2	Stable	3/5/2008	N/A
Thornmint, San Mateo (Acanthomin ha obovata ssp. duttonii)	8	9/18/1985	9/30/1998	F	9/30/1998	180	N/A	N/A	E	6C	Decreasing	N/A	N/A
Townsendia, Last Chance (Townsendia aprica)	6	8/21/1985	8/20/1993	F	8/20/1993	11	N/A	N/A	T	11C	Unknown	N/A	N/A
Trillium, persistent (Trillium persistens)	4	5/27/1978	3/27/1984	F	3/27/1984	20	N/A	N/A	E	8	Stable	7/26/2005	N/A
Trillium, relict (Trillium reliquum)	4	4/4/1988	1/31/1991	F	1/31/1991	16	N/A	N/A	E	8C	Stable	7/26/2005	N/A
Tuctoria, Greene's (Tuctoria greenei)	8	3/26/1997	3/7/2006	F	12/15/2005	192	N/A	N/A	E	2C	Unknown	2/14/2007	1/10/2008
Twinpod, Dudley Bluffs (Physaria obcordata)	6	2/6/1990	8/13/1993	F	8/13/1993	13	N/A	N/A	T	2C	Stable	9/20/2006	6/20/2008
Uluhi (Caesalpinia kavaiense)	1	7/8/1986	5/6/1994	F	5/6/1994	104	N/A	N/A	E	2	Decreasing	4/29/2008	N/A
Uvillo (Eugenia haematocarpa)	4	11/25/1994	9/11/1998	F	9/11/1998	19	N/A	N/A	E	8	Stable	N/A	1/10/2008
Vervain, Red Hills (Verbena californica)	8	9/14/1998	N/A	N/A	N/A	N/A	N/A	N/A	T	14	Unknown	7/7/2005	1/10/2008
Vetch, Hawaiian (Vicia menziesii)	1	5/27/1978	5/18/1984	F	5/18/1984	30	N/A	N/A	E	2C	Decreasing	N/A	N/A
Wahane (Pritchardia aylmer-robinsonii)	1	8/7/1996	N/A	E	N/A	N/A	N/A	N/A	E	5	Stable	N/A	N/A
Wallflower, Ben Lomond (Erysimum teretifolium)	8	2/4/1994	9/28/1998	F	9/28/1998	30	N/A	N/A	E	5	Decreasing	2/14/2007	7/10/2008
Wallflower, Contra Costa (Erysimum capitatum var. angustatum)	8	5/27/1978	3/21/1980	RF(1)	4/25/1984	30	N/A	N/A	E	3	Stable	2/14/2007	7/10/2008
Wallflower, Menzies' (Erysimum menziesii)	8	6/22/1992	9/29/1998	F	9/29/1998	44	N/A	N/A	E	2C	Stable	3/22/2006	7/10/2008

*Earlier drafts and final plans for some individual species may have become incorporated into later multi-species or ecosystem plans.

www.fws.gov/endangered

GENERAL SPECIES INFORMATION					RECOVERY PLAN INFORMATION						SPECIES/RECOVERY STATUS		
Species Name	Lead Region	Date Listed	Date of First Final Plan	Plan Status*	Date of Current or Active Plan	Number of Actions Implemented	Estimated Costs for Recovery	Estimated Time to Recovery (years)	Listing Classification	Recovery Priority Number	FY 2008 Species' Status	Date 5-Year Status Review Initiated	Date 5-Year Status Review Completed
Walnut (=Nogal), West Indian (Juglans jamaicensis)	4	1/13/1997	12/9/1999	F	12/9/1999	19	N/A	N/A	E	5	Unknown	N/A	N/A
Warea, wide-leaf (Warea amplexifolia)	4	4/29/1987	2/17/1993	F	2/17/1993	20	N/A	N/A	E	2C	Decreasing	9/27/2006	9/17/2007
Watercress, Gambel's (Rorippa gambellii)	8	8/3/1993	9/28/1998	F	9/28/1998	40	N/A	N/A	E	2	Decreasing	N/A	N/A
Water-plantain, Kral's (Sagittaria secundifolia)	4	4/13/1990	8/12/1991	F	8/12/1991	16	N/A	N/A	T	8	Stable	9/8/2006	N/A
Water-umbel, Huachuca (Lilaeopsis schaffneriana var. recurva)	2	1/6/1997	N/A	N/A	N/A	N/A	N/A	N/A	E	3C	Stable	N/A	N/A
Water-willow, Cooley's (Jus icia cooleyi)	4	7/27/1989	6/20/1994	F	6/20/1994	23	N/A	N/A	E	8	Decreasing	N/A	N/A
Whitlow-wort, papery (Paronychia chartacea)	4	1/21/1987	5/18/1999	F	5/18/1999	1404	N/A	N/A	T	8	Unknown	4/26/2007	9/28/2008
Wild-buckwheat, clay-loving (Eriogonum pelinophilum)	6	7/13/1984	11/10/1988	F	11/10/1988	15	N/A	N/A	E	2C	Improving	N/A	N/A
Wild-buckwheat, gypsum (Eriogonum gypsophilum)	2	1/19/1981	3/30/1984	F	3/30/1984	7	N/A	N/A	T	8	Stable	2/2/2005	11/9/2007
Wild-buckwheat, southern mountain (Eriogonum kennedyi var. austromontanum)	8	9/14/1998	N/A	N/A	N/A	N/A	N/A	N/A	T	9	Unknown	2/14/2007	3/31/2008
Wild-rice, Texas (Zizania texana)	2	5/27/1978	4/8/1985	RF(1)	2/14/1996	36	N/A	N/A	E	2C	Decreasing	3/20/2008	N/A
Wire-lettuce, Malheur (Stephanomeria malheurensis)	1	11/10/1982	3/21/1991	F	3/21/1991	37	N/A	N/A	E	2	Captivity	N/A	N/A
Wireweed (Polygonella basiramia)	4	1/21/1987	5/18/1999	F	5/18/1999	1404	N/A	N/A	E	2	Unknown	N/A	N/A
Woodland-star, San Clemente Island (Lithophragma maximum)	8	8/8/1997	1/26/1984	F	1/26/1984	54	N/A	N/A	E	2	Stable	7/7/2005	9/24/2007
Woolly-star, Santa Ana River (Eriastrum densifolium ssp. sanctorum)	8	9/28/1987	N/A	N/A	N/A	N/A	N/A	N/A	E	6C	Stable	N/A	N/A
Wooly-threads, San Joaquin (Monolopia (=Lembertia) congdonii)	8	7/19/1990	9/30/1998	F	9/30/1998	223	N/A	N/A	E	1	Unknown	2/14/2007	N/A
Yellowhead, desert (Yermo xanthocephalus)	6	3/14/2002	N/A	N/A	N/A	N/A	N/A	N/A	T	7	Stable	N/A	N/A
Yerba santa, Lompoc (Eriodictyon capitatum)	8	3/20/2000	N/A	N/A	N/A	N/A	N/A	N/A	E	11	Stable	N/A	N/A
Ziziphus, Florida (Ziziphus celata)	4	7/27/1989	5/18/1999	F	5/18/1999	1404	N/A	N/A	E	5	Stable	4/16/2008	N/A
Insects													
Beetle, American burying (Nicrophorus americanus)	2	7/13/1989	9/27/1991	F	9/27/1991	20	N/A	N/A	E	5C	Stable	1/29/2007	6/16/2008
Beetle, Coffin Cave mold (Batrisodes texanus)	2	9/16/1988	8/25/1994	F	8/25/1994	21	N/A	N/A	E	2C	Decreasing	4/23/2007	N/A
Beetle, Comal Springs dryopid (Stygoparnus comalensis)	2	12/18/1997	N/A	N/A	N/A	N/A	N/A	N/A	E	1C	Stable	3/20/2008	N/A
Beetle, Comal Springs riffle (Heterelmis comalensis)	2	12/18/1997	N/A	N/A	N/A	N/A	N/A	N/A	E	2C	Stable	3/20/2008	N/A
Beetle, delta green ground (Elaphus viridis)	8	8/8/1980	9/11/1985	F	12/15/2005	192	N/A	N/A	T	8	Unknown	3/22/2006	N/A
Beetle, Helotes mold (Batrisodes venyivi)	2	12/26/2000	N/A	D	5/16/2008	25	140,628,000	25	E	2C	Stable	4/21/2006	N/A

*Earlier drafts and final plans for some individual species may have become incorporated into later multi-species or ecosystem plans.

Species Name	Lead Region	Date Listed	Date of First Final Plan	Plan Status*	Date of Current or Active Plan	Number of Actions Implemented	Estimated Costs for Recovery	Estimated Time to Recovery (years)	Listing Classification	Recovery Priority Number	FY 2008 Species' Status	Date 5-Year Status Review Initiated	Date 5-Year Status Review Completed
Beetle, Hungerford's crawling water (Brychius hungerfordi)	3	3/7/1994	9/28/2006	F	9/28/2006	27	742,000	24	E	5	Stable	7/19/2005	N/A
Beetle, Kretschmarr Cave mold (Texamaurops reddelli)	2	9/16/1988	8/25/1994	F	8/25/1994	21	N/A	N/A	E	2C	Unknown	4/23/2007	N/A
Beetle, Mount Hermon June (Polyphylla barbata)	8	1/24/1997	9/28/1998	F	9/28/1998	30	N/A	N/A	E	8C	Decreasing	3/5/2008	N/A
Beetle, Tooth Cave ground (Rhadine persephone)	2	9/16/1988	8/25/1994	F	8/25/1994	21	N/A	N/A	E	2C	Stable	8/16/2005	9/30/2008
Beetle, valley elderberry longhorn (Desmocerus californicus dimorphus)	8	8/8/1980	6/28/1984	F	6/28/1984	32	N/A	N/A	T	9C	Stable	7/7/2005	9/26/2006
Butterfly, bay checkerspot (Euphydryas editha bayensis)	8	9/18/1987	9/30/1998	F	9/30/1998	180	N/A	N/A	T	3C	Unknown	3/5/2008	N/A
Butterfly, Behren's silverspot (Speyeria zerene behrensii)	8	12/5/1997	N/A	D	1/20/2004	33	N/A	N/A	E	3C	Unknown	3/22/2006	3/31/2008
Butterfly, callippe silverspot (Speyeria callippe callippe)	8	12/5/1997	N/A	N/A	N/A	N/A	N/A	N/A	E	9C	Unknown	3/5/2008	N/A
Butterfly, El Segundo blue (Euphilotes battoides allyni)	8	6/8/1976	9/28/1998	F	9/28/1998	19	N/A	N/A	E	9	Stable	2/14/2007	3/31/2008
Butterfly, Fender's blue (Icaricia icarioides fenderi)	1	1/25/2000	N/A	D	9/22/2008	73	16,490,000	25	E	3C	Stable	7/6/2005	N/A
Butterfly, Karner blue (Lycaeides melissa samuelis)	3	12/14/1992	9/19/2003	F	9/19/2003	80	N/A	N/A	E	9C	Decreasing	N/A	N/A
Butterfly, Lange's metalmark (Apodemia mormo langei)	8	6/8/1976	3/21/1980	RF(1)	4/25/1984	30	N/A	N/A	E	3	Stable	2/14/2007	7/10/2008
Butterfly, lotis blue (Lycaeides argyrognomon lotis)	8	6/8/1976	12/26/1985	F	12/26/1985	34	N/A	N/A	E	6C	Unknown	2/14/2007	1/10/2008
Butterfly, mission blue (Icaricia icarioides missionensis)	8	6/8/1976	10/10/1984	F	10/10/1984	34	N/A	N/A	E	9	Unknown	3/5/2008	N/A
Butterfly, Mitchell's satyr (Neonympha mitchellii mitchellii)	3	6/25/1991	4/2/1998	F	4/2/1998	47	N/A	N/A	E	3	Stable	N/A	N/A
Butterfly, Myrtle's silverspot (Speyeria zerene myrtleae)	8	6/22/1992	9/29/1998	F	9/29/1998	44	N/A	N/A	E	9	Unknown	3/5/2008	N/A
Butterfly, Oregon silverspot (Speyeria zerene hippolyta)	1	7/2/1980	9/22/1982	RF(1)	8/22/2001	70	13,950,000	19	T	3C	Stable	N/A	N/A
Butterfly, Palos Verdes blue (Glaucopsyche lygdamus palosverdesensis)	8	7/2/1980	1/19/1984	F	1/19/1984	27	N/A	N/A	E	6	Stable	2/14/2007	3/31/2008
Butterfly, Quino checkerspot (Euphydryas editha quino (=E. e. wright))	8	1/16/1997	9/17/2003	F	9/17/2003	33	N/A	N/A	E	3C	Decreasing	9/1/2008	N/A
Butterfly, Saint Francis' satyr (Neonympha mitchellii francisci)	4	4/18/1994	4/23/1996	F	4/23/1996	7	N/A	N/A	E	3	Stable	N/A	N/A
Butterfly, San Bruno elfin (Callophrys mossii bayensis)	8	6/8/1976	10/10/1984	F	10/10/1984	34	N/A	N/A	E	9	Unknown	3/5/2008	N/A
Butterfly, Schaus swallowtail (Heraclides aristodemus ponceanus)	4	4/28/1976	5/18/1999	F	5/18/1999	1404	N/A	N/A	E	3C	Unknown	4/26/2007	9/30/2008

*Earlier drafts and final plans for some individual species may have become incorporated into later multi-species or ecosystem plans.

www.fws.gov/endangered

GENERAL SPECIES INFORMATION			RECOVERY PLAN INFORMATION						SPECIES/RECOVERY STATUS				
Species Name	Lead Region	Date Listed	Date of First Final Plan	Plan Status*	Date of Current or Active Plan	Number of Actions Implemented	Estimated Costs for Recovery	Estimated Time to Recovery (years)	Listing Classifi-cation	Recovery Priority Number	FY 2008 Species' Status	Date 5-Year Status Review Initiated	Date 5-Year Status Review Completed
Butterfly, Smith's blue (Euphilotes enoptes smithi)	8	6/8/1976	11/9/1984	F	11/9/1984	72	N/A	N/A	E	9C	Decreasing	7/7/2005	9/26/2006
Butterfly, Uncompahgre fritillary (Boloria acrocnema)	6	6/24/1991	3/17/1994	F	3/17/1994	22	N/A	N/A	E	8C	Stable	4/18/2007	N/A
Dragonfly, Hine's emerald (Somatochlora hineana)	3	1/26/1995	9/27/2001	F	9/27/2001	76	13,163,000	17	E	5C	Stable	7/27/2007	N/A
Fly, Delhi Sands flower-loving (Rhaphiomidas terminatus abdominalis)	8	9/23/1993	9/14/1997	F	9/14/1997	22	N/A	N/A	E	6C	Unknown	7/7/2005	3/31/2008
Grasshopper, Zayante band-winged (Trimerotropis infantilis)	8	1/24/1997	9/28/1998	F	9/28/1998	30	N/A	N/A	E	2	Decreasing	3/5/2008	N/A
Ground beetle, [unnamed] (Rhadine exilis)	2	12/26/2000	N/A	D	5/16/2008	25	140,628,000	25	E	2C	Decreasing	4/21/2006	N/A
Ground beetle, [unnamed] (Rhadine infernalis)	2	12/26/2000	N/A	D	5/16/2008	25	140,628,000	25	E	2C	Decreasing	4/21/2006	N/A
Moth, Blackburn's sphinx (Manduca blackburni)	1	2/1/2000	9/28/2005	F	9/28/2005	25	5,580,000	N/A	E	2C	Stable	3/8/2007	N/A
Moth, Kern primrose sphinx (Euproserpinus euterpe)	8	4/8/1980	2/8/1984	F	2/8/1984	26	N/A	N/A	T	2	Unknown	2/22/2006	9/24/2007
Naucorid, Ash Meadows (Ambrysus amargosus)	8	5/20/1985	9/28/1990	F	9/28/1990	82	N/A	N/A	T	8	Stable	3/5/2008	N/A
Pomace fly, [unnamed] (Drosophila aglaia)	1	5/9/2006	N/A	N/A	N/A	N/A	N/A	N/A	E	5	Decreasing	N/A	N/A
Pomace fly, [unnamed] (Drosophila differens)	1	5/9/2006	N/A	N/A	N/A	N/A	N/A	N/A	E	5	Decreasing	N/A	N/A
Pomace fly, [unnamed] (Drosophila hemipeza)	1	5/9/2006	N/A	N/A	N/A	N/A	N/A	N/A	E	5	Decreasing	N/A	N/A
Pomace fly, [unnamed] (Drosophila heteroneura)	1	5/9/2006	N/A	N/A	N/A	N/A	N/A	N/A	E	5	Decreasing	N/A	N/A
Pomace fly, [unnamed] (Drosophila montgomeryi)	1	5/9/2006	N/A	N/A	N/A	N/A	N/A	N/A	E	5	Decreasing	N/A	N/A
Pomace fly, [unnamed] (Drosophila mulli)	1	5/9/2006	N/A	N/A	N/A	N/A	N/A	N/A	T	5	Decreasing	N/A	N/A
Pomace fly, [unnamed] (Drosophila musaphila)	1	5/9/2006	N/A	N/A	N/A	N/A	N/A	N/A	E	5	Decreasing	N/A	N/A
Pomace fly, [unnamed] (Drosophila neoclavisetae)	1	5/9/2006	N/A	N/A	N/A	N/A	N/A	N/A	E	5	Decreasing	N/A	N/A
Pomace fly, [unnamed] (Drosophila obatai)	1	5/9/2006	N/A	N/A	N/A	N/A	N/A	N/A	E	5	Decreasing	N/A	N/A
Pomace fly, [unnamed] (Drosophila ochrobasis)	1	5/9/2006	N/A	N/A	N/A	N/A	N/A	N/A	E	5	Decreasing	N/A	N/A
Pomace fly, [unnamed] (Drosophila substenoptera)	1	5/9/2006	N/A	N/A	N/A	N/A	N/A	N/A	E	5	Decreasing	N/A	N/A
Pomace fly, [unnamed] (Drosophila tarphytrichia)	1	5/9/2006	N/A	N/A	N/A	N/A	N/A	N/A	E	5	Decreasing	N/A	N/A
Skipper, Carson wandering (Pseudocopaeodes eunus obscurus)	8	11/29/2001	9/13/2007	F	9/13/2007	34	N/A	N/A	E	3C	Stable	3/5/2008	N/A

*Earlier drafts and final plans for some individual species may have become incorporated into later multi-species or ecosystem plans.

www.fws.gov/endangered

Recovery Data as of September 30, 2008

GENERAL SPECIES INFORMATION			RECOVERY PLAN INFORMATION						SPECIES/RECOVERY STATUS				
Species Name	Lead Region	Date Listed	Date of First Final Plan	Plan Status*	Date of Current or Active Plan	Number of Actions Implemented	Estimated Costs for Recovery	Estimated Time to Recovery (years)	Listing Classification	Recovery Priority Number	FY 2008 Species' Status	Date 5-Year Status Review Initiated	Date 5-Year Status Review Completed
Skipper, Laguna Mountains (Pyrgus ruralis lagunae)	8	1/16/1997	N/A	N/A	N/A	N/A	N/A	N/A	E	3C	Decreasing	3/22/2006	9/24/2007
Skipper, Pawnee montane (Hesperia leonardus montana)	6	9/25/1987	9/21/1998	F	9/21/1998	13	330,000	12	T	9C	Improving	N/A	N/A
Tiger beetle, northeastern beach (Cicindela dorsalis dorsalis)	5	8/7/1990	9/29/1994	F	9/29/1994	19	476,000	11	T	6	Decreasing	1/16/2008	N/A
Tiger beetle, Ohlone (Cicindela ohlone)	8	10/3/2001	9/28/1998	F	9/28/1998	30	N/A	N/A	E	2	Decreasing	N/A	N/A
Tiger beetle, Puritan (Cicindela puritana)	5	8/7/1990	9/29/1993	F	9/29/1993	22	632,500	15	T	5	Decreasing	4/21/2006	6/13/2007
Tiger beetle, Salt Creek (Cicindela nevadica lincolniana)	6	10/6/2005	N/A	N/A	N/A	N/A	N/A	N/A	E	3C	Decreasing	N/A	N/A
Lichens													
Cladonia, Florida perforate (Cladonia perforata)	4	4/27/1993	5/18/1999	F	5/18/1999	1404	N/A	N/A	E	5C	Unknown	9/27/2006	9/17/2007
Lichen, rock gnome (Gymnoderma lineare)	4	1/18/1995	9/30/1997	F	9/30/1997	16	N/A	N/A	E	5	Unknown	9/21/2007	N/A
Mammals													
Bat, gray (Myotis grisescens)	3	4/28/1976	7/8/1982	F	7/8/1982	44	N/A	N/A	E	8	Stable	3/30/2006	N/A
Bat, Hawaiian hoary (Lasiurus cinereus semotus)	1	10/13/1970	5/11/1998	F	5/11/1998	13	N/A	N/A	E	9	Unknown	N/A	N/A
Bat, Indiana (Myotis sodalis)	3	3/11/1967	10/14/1983	RD(1)	4/13/2007	116	N/A	N/A	E	8	Decreasing	9/21/2006	N/A
Bat, lesser long-nosed (Leptonycteris curasoae yerbabuenae)	2	9/30/1988	3/4/1997	F	3/4/1997	22	N/A	N/A	E	8	Stable	2/2/2005	9/11/2007
Bat, little Mariana fruit (Pteropus tokudae)	1	8/27/1984	11/2/1990	F	11/2/1990	107	N/A	N/A	E	5	Presumed Extinct	3/8/2007	N/A
Bat, Mariana fruit (=Mariana flying fox) (Pteropus mariannus mariannus)	1	8/27/1984	11/2/1990	F	11/2/1990	N/A	N/A	N/A	T	9	Decreasing	7/6/2005	9/4/2007
Bat, Mexican long-nosed (Leptonycteris nivalis)	2	9/30/1988	9/8/1994	F	9/8/1994	31	N/A	N/A	E	5	Unknown	N/A	N/A
Bat, Ozark big-eared (Corynorhinus (=Plecotus) townsendii ingens)	2	11/30/1979	5/8/1984	RF(1)	3/28/1995	26	N/A	N/A	E	3	Stable	4/21/2006	5/22/2008
Bat, Virginia big-eared (Corynorhinus (=Plecotus) townsendii virginianus)	5	12/31/1979	5/8/1984	F	5/8/1984	45	N/A	N/A	E	9C	Stable	1/29/2007	8/27/2008
Bear, grizzly (Ursus arctos horribilis)	6	3/11/1967	1/29/1982	RF(1)	9/10/1993	296	N/A	N/A	T	3C	Improving	4/18/2007	N/A
Bear, Louisiana black (Ursus americanus luteolus)	4	1/7/1992	9/27/1995	F	9/27/1995	21	N/A	N/A	T	9	Improving	8/2/2007	N/A
Bear, polar (Ursus maritimus)	7	5/15/2008	N/A	N/A	N/A	N/A	N/A	N/A	T	UNK	Unknown	N/A	N/A
Caribou, woodland (Rangifer tarandus caribou)	1	1/14/1983	4/12/1985	RF(2)	3/4/1994	63	N/A	N/A	E	3C	Decreasing	4/11/2006	N/A
Deer, Columbian white-tailed (Odocoileus virginianus leucurus)	1	3/11/1967	10/21/1976	RF(1)	6/14/1983	28	N/A	N/A	E	9	Stable	N/A	N/A
Deer, key (Odocoileus virginianus clavium)	4	3/11/1967	5/18/1999	F	5/18/1999	1404	N/A	N/A	E	6C	Stable	6/21/2005	N/A
Ferret, black-footed (Mustela nigripes)	6	3/11/1967	6/14/1978	RF(1)	8/8/1988	190	N/A	N/A	E	2C	Improving	7/7/2005	12/1/2008
Fox, San Joaquin kit (Vulpes macrotis mutica)	8	3/11/1967	9/30/1998	F	9/30/1998	223	N/A	N/A	E	3C	Decreasing	3/22/2006	N/A

*Earlier drafts and final plans for some individual species may have become incorporated into later multi-species or ecosystem plans.

www.fws.gov/endangered

Recovery Data as of September 30, 2008

Species Name	Lead Region	Date Listed	Date of First Final Plan	Plan Status*	Date of Current or Active Plan	Number of Actions Implemented	Estimated Costs for Recovery	Estimated Time to Recovery (years)	Listing Classification	Recovery Priority Number	FY 2008 Species' Status	Date 5-Year Status Review Initiated	Date 5-Year Status Review Completed
Fox, San Miguel Island (Urocyon littoralis littoralis)	8	3/5/2004	N/A	N/A	N/A	N/A	N/A	N/A	E	3	Improving	N/A	N/A
Fox, Santa Catalina Island (Urocyon littoralis catalinae)	8	3/5/2004	N/A	N/A	N/A	N/A	N/A	N/A	E	9	Improving	N/A	N/A
Fox, Santa Cruz Island (Urocyon littoralis santacruzae)	8	3/5/2004	N/A	N/A	N/A	N/A	N/A	N/A	E	3	Stable	N/A	N/A
Fox, Santa Rosa Island (Urocyon littoralis santarosae)	8	3/5/2004	N/A	N/A	N/A	N/A	N/A	N/A	E	3	Stable	N/A	N/A
Jaguar (Panthera onca)	2	3/28/1972	8/22/1990	E	N/A	N/A	N/A	N/A	E	5C	Unknown	4/21/2006	N/A
Jaguarundi, Gulf Coast (Herpailurus (=Felis) yagouaroundi cacomitli)	2	6/14/1976	8/22/1990	F	8/22/1990	80	N/A	N/A	E	6	Unknown	N/A	N/A
Jaguarundi, Sinaloan (Herpailurus (=Felis) yagouaroundi tolteca)	2	6/14/1976	N/A	E	N/A	N/A	N/A	N/A	E	6	Unknown	N/A	N/A
Kangaroo rat, Fresno (Dipodomys nitratoides exilis)	8	1/30/1985	9/30/1998	F	9/30/1998	223	N/A	N/A	E	3C	Unknown	3/22/2006	N/A
Kangaroo rat, giant (Dipodomys ingens)	8	1/5/1987	9/30/1998	F	9/30/1998	223	N/A	N/A	E	2C	Stable	3/22/2006	N/A
Kangaroo rat, Morro Bay (Dipodomys heermanni morroensis)	8	10/13/1970	4/18/1982	RD(1)	1/25/2000	68	N/A	N/A	E	6C	Decreasing	N/A	N/A
Kangaroo rat, San Bernardino Merriam's (Dipodomys merriami parvus)	8	1/27/1998	N/A	N/A	N/A	N/A	N/A	N/A	E	6C	Unknown	3/5/2008	N/A
Kangaroo rat, Stephens' (Dipodomys stephensi (incl. D. cascus))	8	9/30/1988	N/A	D	6/23/1997	25	N/A	N/A	E	2C	Unknown	4/21/2004	N/A
Kangaroo rat, Tipton (Dipodomys nitratoides nitratoides)	8	7/8/1988	9/30/1998	F	9/30/1998	223	N/A	N/A	E	3C	Stable	2/14/2007	N/A
Lynx, Canada (Lynx canadensis)	6	3/24/2000	N/A	N/A	N/A	N/A	N/A	N/A	T	15	Stable	4/18/2007	N/A
Manatee, West Indian (Trichechus manatus)	4	3/11/1967	4/15/1980	RF(3), F	12/24/1986, 10/30/2001	132	10,000,000	14	E	5C	Stable	4/15/2005	4/6/2007
Mountain beaver, Point Arena (Aplodonia rufa nigra)	8	12/12/1991	6/2/1998	F	6/2/1998	34	N/A	N/A	E	9C	Unknown	3/5/2008	N/A
Mouse, Alabama beach (Peromyscus polionotus ammobates)	4	6/6/1985	8/12/1987	F	8/12/1987	64	N/A	N/A	E	3C	Unknown	9/8/2006	N/A
Mouse, Anastasia Island beach (Peromyscus polionotus phasma)	4	5/12/1989	9/23/1993	F	9/23/1993	15	133,000	9	E	6C	Stable	9/27/2006	9/6/2007
Mouse, Choctawhatchee beach (Peromyscus polionotus allophrys)	4	6/6/1985	8/12/1987	F	8/12/1987	64	N/A	N/A	E	3C	Improving	9/27/2006	9/4/2007
Mouse, Key Largo cotton (Peromyscus gossypinus allapaticola)	4	9/21/1983	5/18/1999	F	5/18/1999	1404	N/A	N/A	E	3C	Stable	4/16/2008	N/A
Mouse, Pacific pocket (Perognathus longimembris pacificus)	8	2/3/1994	9/28/1998	F	9/28/1998	42	N/A	N/A	E	3C	Decreasing	2/14/2007	N/A
Mouse, Perdido Key beach (Peromyscus polionotus trissyllepsis)	4	6/6/1985	8/12/1987	F	8/12/1987	64	N/A	N/A	E	3C	Decreasing	9/27/2006	9/4/2007
Mouse, Preble's meadow jumping (Zapus hudsonius preblei)	6	5/13/1998	N/A	N/A	N/A	N/A	N/A	N/A	T	9C	Decreasing	3/31/2004	2/1/2008
Mouse, salt marsh harvest (Reithrodontomys raviventris)	8	10/13/1970	11/16/1984	F	11/16/1984	69	N/A	N/A	E	2C	Unknown	3/5/2008	N/A

GENERAL SPECIES INFORMATION | RECOVERY PLAN INFORMATION | SPECIES/RECOVERY STATUS

*Earlier drafts and final plans for some individual species may
have become incorporated into later multi-species or ecosystem plans.

www.fws.gov/endangered

Species Name	Lead Region	Date Listed	Date of First Final Plan	Plan Status*	Date of Current or Active Plan	Number of Actions Implemented	Estimated Costs for Recovery	Estimated Time to Recovery (years)	Listing Classification	Recovery Priority Number	FY 2008 Species' Status	Date 5-Year Status Review Initiated	Date 5-Year Status Review Completed
GENERAL SPECIES INFORMATION						**RECOVERY PLAN INFORMATION**			**SPECIES/RECOVERY STATUS**				
Mouse, southeastern beach (Peromyscus polionotus niveiventris)	4	5/12/1989	9/23/1993	F	9/23/1993	15	133,000	9	T	9C	Stable	4/26/2007	4/7/2008
Mouse, St. Andrew beach (Peromyscus polionotus peninsularis)	4	12/18/1998	N/A	N/A	N/A	N/A	N/A	N/A	E	3C	Stable	6/21/2005	N/A
Ocelot (Leopardus (=Felis) pardalis)	2	3/28/1972	8/22/1990	F	8/22/1990	80	N/A	N/A	E	5C	Decreasing	N/A	N/A
Otter, Northern Sea (Enhydra lutris kenyoni)	7	8/9/2005	N/A	N/A	N/A	N/A	N/A	N/A	T	6	Unknown	N/A	N/A
Otter, southern sea (Enhydra lutris nereis)	8	1/14/1977	2/3/1982	RF(1)	4/3/2003	24	N/A	N/A	T	9C	Stable	N/A	N/A
Panther, Florida	4	3/11/1967	12/17/1981	RD(3)	1/31/2006	N/A	17,750	75	E	6C	Decreasing	6/21/2005	N/A
Prairie dog, Utah (Cynomys parvidens)	6	6/4/1973	9/30/1991	F	9/30/1991	27	950,000	9	T	8C	Stable	2/21/2007	N/A
Pronghorn, Sonoran (Antilocapra americana sonoriensis)	2	3/11/1967	12/30/1982	RF(1)	11/26/2003, 12/03/1998	48	N/A	N/A	E	3	Stable	3/20/2008	N/A
Puma (=cougar), eastern (Puma (=Felis) concolor couguar)	5	6/4/1973	8/2/1982	F	8/2/1982	4	N/A	N/A	E	18	Presumed Extinct	1/29/2007	N/A
Rabbit, Lower Keys marsh (Sylvilagus palustris hefneri)	4	6/21/1990	5/18/1999	F	5/18/1999	1404	N/A	N/A	E	6C	Stable	9/27/2006	9/21/2007
Rabbit, pygmy (Brachylagus idahoensis)	1	11/30/2001	N/A	D	9/7/2007	32	N/A	N/A	E	3	Decreasing	N/A	N/A
Rabbit, riparian brush (Sylvilagus bachmani riparius)	8	2/23/2000	9/30/1998	F	9/30/1998	223	N/A	N/A	E	6C	Stable	N/A	N/A
Rice rat (Oryzomys palustris natator)	4	4/30/1991	5/18/1999	F	5/18/1999	1404	N/A	N/A	E	3C	Stable	4/26/2007	8/18/2008
Sheep, bighorn (Ovis canadensis)	8	3/18/1998	10/25/2000	F	10/25/2000	45	N/A	N/A	E	3C	Stable	N/A	N/A
Sheep, Sierra Nevada bighorn (Ovis canadensis sierrae)	8	4/20/1999	2/13/2008	F	2/13/2008	30	21,730,000	20	E	3C	Improving	2/14/2007	9/30/2008
Shrew, Buena Vista Lake ornate (Sorex ornatus relictus)	8	3/6/2002	9/30/1998	F	9/30/1998	223	N/A	N/A	E	3C	Unknown	N/A	N/A
Squirrel, Carolina northern flying (Glaucomys sabrinus coloratus)	4	7/1/1985	9/24/1990	F	9/24/1990	21	N/A	N/A	E	6C	Stable	9/21/2007	N/A
Squirrel, Delmarva Peninsula fox (Sciurus niger cinereus)	5	3/11/1967	11/6/1979	RF(2)	6/8/1993	34	784,100	17	E	15C	Improving	7/6/2005	9/30/2007
Squirrel, Mount Graham red (Tamiasciurus hudsonicus grahamensis)	2	6/3/1987	5/3/1993	F	5/3/1993	34	N/A	N/A	E	6C	Decreasing	1/11/2006	1/15/2008
Squirrel, northern Idaho ground (Spermophilus brunneus brunneus)	1	4/5/2000	9/16/2003	F	9/16/2003	49	2,440,000	8	T	3C	Stable	N/A	N/A
Vole, Amargosa (Microtus californicus scirpensis)	8	11/15/1984	9/15/1997	F	9/15/1997	37	N/A	N/A	E	6	Unknown	3/5/2008	N/A
Vole, Florida salt marsh (Microtus pennsylvanicus dukecampbelli)	4	1/14/1991	9/30/1997	F	9/30/1997	8	N/A	N/A	E	6	Unknown	4/26/2007	6/5/2008
Vole, Hualapai Mexican (Microtus mexicanus hualpaiensis)	2	10/1/1987	8/19/1991	F	8/19/1991	25	N/A	N/A	E	4	Unknown	N/A	N/A
Wolf, gray (Minnesota) (Canis lupus)	3	4/10/1978	6/5/1978	RF(1)	1/31/1992	66	13,500,000	13	T	14C	Stable	N/A	N/A
Wolf, gray (lower 48 States and Mexico) (Canis lupus)	6	3/11/1967	5/28/1980	RF(1)	8/3/1987	33	N/A	N/A	E	15C	Improving	9/20/2005	N/A
Wolf, red (Canis rufus)	4	3/11/1967	7/12/1982	RF(2)	10/26/1990	40	N/A	N/A	E	5C	Decreasing	9/20/2005	9/28/2007

*Earlier drafts and final plans for some individual species may have become incorporated into later multi-species or ecosystem plans.

www.fws.gov/endangered

GENERAL SPECIES INFORMATION			RECOVERY PLAN INFORMATION						SPECIES/RECOVERY STATUS				
Species Name	Lead Region	Date Listed	Date of First Final Plan	Plan Status*	Date of Current or Active Plan	Number of Actions Implemented	Estimated Costs for Recovery	Estimated Time to Recovery (years)	Listing Classifi-cation	Recovery Priority Number	FY 2008 Species' Status	Date 5-Year Status Review Initiated	Date 5-Year Status Review Completed
Woodrat, Key Largo (Neotoma floridana smalli)	4	9/21/1983	5/18/1999	F	5/18/1999	1404	N/A	N/A	E	3C	Decreasing	4/26/2007	9/25/2008
Woodrat, riparian (=San Joaquin Valley) (Neotoma fuscipes riparia)	8	2/23/2000	9/30/1998	F	9/30/1998	223	N/A	N/A	E	6C	Stable	N/A	N/A
Reptiles													
Anole, Culebra Island giant (Anolis roosevelti)	4	8/22/1977	1/28/1983	F	1/28/1983	3	N/A	N/A	E	17	Presumed Extinct	9/27/2006	N/A
Boa, Mona (Epicrates monensis monensis)	4	3/6/1978	4/19/1984	F	4/19/1984	9	N/A	N/A	T	3	Stable	9/21/2007	N/A
Boa, Puerto Rican (Epicrates inornatus)	4	10/13/1970	3/27/1986	F	3/27/1986	12	N/A	N/A	E	14C	Stable	9/12/2005	N/A
Boa, Virgin Islands tree (Epicrates monensis granti)	4	10/13/1970	3/27/1986	F	3/27/1986	13	N/A	N/A	E	9C	Stable	9/12/2005	N/A
Crocodile, American (Crocodylus acutus)	4	10/28/1975	5/18/1999	F	5/18/1999	1404	N/A	N/A	T	2C	Stable	3/24/2005	3/20/2007
Gecko, Monito (Sphaerodactylus micropithecus)	4	10/15/1982	3/27/1986	F	3/27/1986	11	N/A	N/A	E	5	Stable	9/21/2007	N/A
Iguana, Mona ground (Cyclura cornuta stejnegeri)	4	3/6/1978	4/19/1984	F	4/19/1984	13	N/A	N/A	T	3	Stable	9/21/2007	N/A
Lizard, blunt-nosed leopard (Gambelia silus)	8	3/11/1967	9/30/1998	F	9/30/1998	223	N/A	N/A	E	2C	Stable	3/22/2006	N/A
Lizard, Coachella Valley fringe-toed (Uma inornata)	8	9/25/1980	9/11/1985	F	9/11/1985	44	N/A	N/A	T	5C	Decreasing	2/14/2007	N/A
Lizard, Island night (Xantusia riversiana)	8	9/12/1977	1/26/1984	F	1/26/1984	54	N/A	N/A	T	8	Stable	7/7/2005	9/26/2006
Lizard, St. Croix ground (Ameiva polops)	4	7/5/1977	3/29/1984	F	3/29/1984	9	N/A	N/A	E	8	Improving	9/21/2007	N/A
Plymouth Red-Bellied Cooter (Pseudemys rubriventris bangsi)	5	4/2/1980	1/1/1981	RF(2)	5/6/1994	18	421,500	17	E	9	Stable	4/21/2006	9/30/2007
Rat lesnake, New Mexican ridge-nosed (Crotalus willardi obscurus)	2	8/21/1978	3/22/1985	F	3/22/1985	22	N/A	N/A	T	3	Unknown	4/23/2007	N/A
Sea turtle, green (FL, Mexico nesting populations) (Chelonia mydas)	4	7/28/1978	9/19/1984	RF(1)	1/12/1998	111	145,700,000	23	E	1C	Improving	4/21/2005	8/22/2007
Sea turtle, green (except where endangered) (Chelonia mydas)	4	7/28/1978	9/19/1984	RF(1)	1/12/1998	N/A	N/A	N/A	T	1C	Unknown	4/21/2005	8/22/2007
Sea turtle, hawksbill (Eretmochelys imbricata)	4	6/2/1970	9/19/1984	RF(1)	01/12/1998, 12/15/1993	89	12,850,000	26	E	1C	Unknown	4/21/2005	8/23/2007
Sea turtle, Kemp's ridley (Lepidochelys kempii)	2	12/2/1970	9/19/1984	RF(1)	8/21/1992, 04/06/1992	25	N/A	N/A	E	2C	Improving	4/21/2005	8/24/2007
Sea turtle, leatherback (Dermochelys coriacea)	4	6/2/1970	9/19/1984	RF(1)	01/12/1998	94	6,740,000	23	E	1	Decreasing	4/21/2005	8/21/2007
Sea turtle, loggerhead (Caretta caretta)	4	7/28/1978	9/19/1984	RF(1)	01/12/1998	50	N/A	N/A	T	7C	Unknown	4/21/2005	8/27/2007
Sea turtle, olive ridley (except where endangered) (Lepidochelys olivacea)	4	7/28/1978	9/19/1984	RF(1)	1/12/1998	42	N/A	N/A	T	8C	Unknown	4/21/2005	8/21/2007
Sea turtle, olive ridley (Mexican nesting population) (Lepidochelys olivacea)	4	7/28/1978	9/19/1984	RF(1)	1/12/1998	42	N/A	N/A	E	8C	Improving	4/21/2005	8/21/2007
Skink, bluetail mole (Eumeces egregius lividus)	4	11/6/1987	5/18/1999	F	5/18/1999	1404	N/A	N/A	T	3C	Unknown	9/27/2006	8/2/2007

*Earlier drafts and final plans for some individual species may
have become incorporated into later multi-species or ecosystem plans.

www.fws.gov/endangered

	GENERAL SPECIES INFORMATION				RECOVERY PLAN INFORMATION						SPECIES/RECOVERY STATUS		
Species Name	Lead Region	Date Listed	Date of First Final Plan	Plan Status*	Date of Current or Active Plan	Number of Actions Implemented	Estimated Costs for Recovery	Estimated Time to Recovery (years)	Listing Classifi-cation	Recovery Priority Number	FY 2008 Species' Status	Date 5-Year Status Review Initiated	Date 5-Year Status Review Completed
Skink, sand (Neoseps reynoldsi)	4	11/6/1987	5/18/1999	F	5/18/1999	1404	N/A	N/A	T	1C	Unknown	9/27/2006	8/2/2007
Snake, Atlantic salt marsh (Nerodia clarkii taeniata)	4	12/29/1977	12/15/1993	F	12/15/1993	13	152,000	7	T	12	Unknown	4/26/2007	3/24/2008
Snake, Concho water (Nerodia paucimaculata)	2	9/3/1986	9/27/1993	F	9/27/1993	12	2,729,000	12	T	14	Improving	N/A	N/A
Snake, copperbelly water (Nerodia erythrogaster neglecta)	3	1/29/1997	N/A	D	9/6/2007	34	N/A	N/A	T	3C	Decreasing	6/2/2006	N/A
Snake, eastern indigo (Drymarchon corais couperi)	4	3/3/1978	4/22/1982	F	4/22/1982	18	N/A	N/A	T	11C	Unknown	9/8/2006	4/29/2008
Snake, giant garter (Thamnophis gigas)	8	10/20/1993	N/A	D	7/2/1999	52	N/A	N/A	T	2C	Decreasing	7/7/2005	9/26/2006
Snake, San Francisco garter (Thamnophis sirtalis tetrataenia)	8	3/11/1967	9/11/1985	F	9/11/1985	53	N/A	N/A	E	3C	Stable	7/7/2005	9/26/2006
Tortoise, desert (Gopherus agassizii)	8	8/20/1980	6/28/1994	RD(1)	8/4/2008	39	159,000,000	17	T	6C	Decreasing	N/A	N/A
Tortoise, gopher (Gopherus polyphemus)	4	7/7/1987	12/26/1990	F	12/26/1990	15	N/A	N/A	T	9	Decreasing	N/A	N/A
Turtle, Alabama red-belly (Pseudemys alabamensis)	4	6/16/1987	1/8/1990	F	1/8/1990	11	N/A	N/A	E	5	Unknown	8/2/2007	N/A
Turtle, bog (=Muhlenberg) (Clemmys muhlenbergii)	5	11/4/1997	5/15/2001	F	5/15/2001	58	1,863,000	49	T	5C	Stable	1/29/2007	N/A
Turtle, flattened musk (Sternotherus depressus)	4	6/11/1987	2/26/1990	F	2/26/1990	8	N/A	N/A	T	14	Unknown	N/A	N/A
Turtle, ringed map (Graptemys oculifera)	4	12/23/1986	4/8/1988	F	4/8/1988	13	N/A	N/A	T	14	Unknown	6/14/2005	N/A
Turtle, yellow-blotched map (Graptemys flavimaculata)	4	1/14/1991	3/15/1993	F	3/15/1993	6	N/A	N/A	T	14	Unknown	N/A	N/A
Watersnake, Lake Erie (Nerodia sipedon insularum)	3	8/30/1999	9/25/2003	F	9/25/2003	36	960,000	10	T	3C	Improving	4/22/2008	N/A
Whipsnake (=striped racer), Alameda (Masticophis lateralis euryxanthus)	8	12/5/1997	N/A	D	4/7/2003	211	N/A	N/A	T	9C	Stable	N/A	N/A
Snails													
Ambersnail, Kanab (Oxyloma haydeni kanabensis)	6	8/8/1991	10/12/1995	F	10/12/1995	23	N/A	N/A	E	6C	Stable	4/7/2006	N/A
Campeloma, slender (Campeloma decampi)	4	2/25/2000	N/A	N/A	N/A	N/A	N/A	N/A	E	5	Stable	8/2/2007	N/A
Cavesnail, Tumbling Creek (Antrobia culveri)	3	8/14/2002	9/22/2003	F	9/22/2003	77	2,174,000	20	E	4	Stable	N/A	N/A
Elimia, lacy (snail) (Elimia crenatella)	4	10/28/1998	12/2/2005	F	12/2/2005	28	N/A	N/A	T	8	Unknown	6/14/2005	8/29/2006
Limpet, Banbury Springs (Lanx sp.)	1	12/14/1992	11/26/1995	F	11/26/1995	47	N/A	N/A	E	6	Stable	4/11/2006	9/15/2006
Lioplax, cylindrical (snail) (Lioplax cyclostomaformis)	4	10/28/1998	12/2/2005	F	12/2/2005	28	N/A	N/A	E	8	Improving	6/14/2005	8/29/2006
Marstonia, royal (snail) (Pyrgulopsis ogmorhaphe)	4	4/15/1994	8/11/1995	F	8/11/1995	13	N/A	N/A	E	5	Decreasing	7/28/2006	N/A
Pebblesnail, flat (Lepyrium showalteri)	4	10/28/1998	12/2/2005	F	12/2/2005	28	N/A	N/A	E	5	Unknown	6/14/2005	8/29/2006
Riversnail, Anthony's (Atheamia anthonyi)	4	4/15/1994	8/13/1997	F	8/13/1997	13	422,500	N/A	E	5	Stable	N/A	N/A
Rocksnail, painted (Leptoxis taeniata)	4	10/28/1998	12/2/2005	F	12/2/2005	28	N/A	N/A	T	8	Unknown	6/14/2005	8/29/2006

*Earlier drafts and final plans for some individual species may have become incorporated into later multi-species or ecosystem plans.

www.fws.gov/endangered

GENERAL SPECIES INFORMATION			RECOVERY PLAN INFORMATION						SPECIES/RECOVERY STATUS				
Species Name	Lead Region	Date Listed	Date of First Final Plan	Plan Status*	Date of Current or Active Plan	Number of Actions Implemented	Estimated Costs for Recovery	Estimated Time to Recovery (years)	Listing Classification	Recovery Priority Number	FY 2008 Species' Status	Date 5-Year Status Review Initiated	Date 5-Year Status Review Completed
Rocksnail, plicate (Leptoxis plicata)	4	10/28/1998	12/2/2005	F	12/2/2005	28	N/A	N/A	E	5C	Stable	6/14/2005	8/29/2006
Rocksnail, round (Leptoxis ampla)	4	10/28/1998	12/2/2005	F	12/2/2005	28	N/A	N/A	T	8	Unknown	6/14/2005	8/29/2006
Shagreen, Magazine Mountain (Mesodon magazinensis)	4	4/17/1989	2/1/1994	F	2/1/1994	7	N/A	N/A	T	8	Stable	N/A	N/A
Snail, armored (Pyrgulopsis (=Marstonia) pachyta)	4	2/25/2000	N/A	D	7/1/1994	N/A	N/A	N/A	E	5	Unknown	8/2/2007	N/A
Snail, Bliss Rapids (Taylorconcha serpenticola)	1	12/14/1992	11/26/1995	F	11/26/1995	47	N/A	N/A	T	7C	Stable	7/27/2004	N/A
Snail, Chittenango ovate amber (Succinea chittenangoensis)	5	8/2/1978	3/24/1983	RF(1)	8/21/2006	39	N/A	N/A	T	5	Stable	7/6/2005	10/4/2006
Snail, flat-spired three-toothed (Triodopsis platysayoides)	5	8/2/1978	5/9/1983	F	5/9/1983	12	N/A	N/A	T	8C	Decreasing	4/21/2006	11/6/2007
Snail, Iowa Pleistocene (Discus macclintocki)	3	8/2/1978	3/22/1984	F	3/22/1984	12	N/A	N/A	E	14	Stable	3/30/2006	N/A
Snail, Morro shoulderband (=Banded dune) (Helminthoglypta walkeriana)	8	12/15/1994	9/28/1998	F	9/28/1998	36	N/A	N/A	E	8C	Stable	7/7/2005	9/11/2006
Snail, Newcomb's (Erinna newcombi)	1	1/26/2000	9/18/2006	F	9/18/2006	23	2,530,000	14	T	1	Unknown	3/8/2007	N/A
Snail, noonday (Mesodon clarki nantahala)	4	8/2/1978	9/7/1984	F	9/7/1984	15	N/A	N/A	T	9	Decreasing	9/21/2007	N/A
Snail, Oahu tree (Achatinella spp.)	1	2/12/1981	6/30/1992	F	6/30/1992	44	N/A	N/A	E	2	Unknown	N/A	N/A
Snail, painted snake coiled forest (Anguispira picta)	4	8/2/1978	10/14/1982	F	10/14/1982	14	N/A	N/A	T	8C	Stable	9/20/2005	1/16/2008
Snail, Pecos assiminea (Assiminea pecos)	2	8/9/2005	N/A	N/A	N/A	N/A	N/A	N/A	E	5	Stable	N/A	N/A
Snail, Snake River physa (Physa natricina)	1	12/14/1992	11/26/1995	F	11/26/1995	47	N/A	N/A	E	5C	Improving	N/A	N/A
Snail, Stock Island tree (Orthalicus reses (not incl. nesodryas))	4	8/2/1978	5/18/1999	F	5/18/1999	1404	N/A	N/A	T	3	Unknown	4/16/2008	N/A
Snail, tulotoma (Tulotoma magnifica)	4	1/9/1991	11/17/2000	F	11/17/2000	29	N/A	N/A	E	8	Stable	6/14/2005	2/29/2008
Snail, Utah valvata (Valvata utahensis)	1	12/14/1992	11/26/1995	F	11/26/1995	47	N/A	N/A	E	5C	Stable	4/11/2006	N/A
Snail, Virginia fringed mountain (Polygyriscus virginianus)	5	8/2/1978	5/9/1983	F	5/9/1983	14	N/A	N/A	E	4	Unknown	8/29/2007	1/29/2008
Springsnail, Alamosa (Tryonia alamosae)	2	9/30/1991	8/31/1994	F	8/31/1994	15	N/A	N/A	E	14	Stable	N/A	N/A
Springsnail, Bruneau Hot (Pyrgulopsis bruneauensis)	1	1/25/1993	9/30/2002	F	9/30/2002	28	15,000,000	15	E	2C	Decreasing	4/11/2006	6/24/2007
Springsnail, Koster's (Juturnia kosteri)	2	8/9/2005	N/A	N/A	N/A	N/A	N/A	N/A	E	5	Stable	N/A	N/A
Springsnail, Roswell (Pyrgulopsis roswellensis)	2	8/9/2005	N/A	N/A	N/A	N/A	N/A	N/A	E	5	Stable	N/A	N/A
Springsnail, Socorro (Pyrgulopsis neomexicana)	2	9/30/1991	8/31/1994	F	8/31/1994	15	N/A	N/A	E	5	Unknown	3/20/2008	N/A

*Earlier drafts and final plans for some individual species may have become incorporated into later multi-species or ecosystem plans.

www.fws.gov/endangered

Endangered Species Program Contacts

Washington D.C. Office
Endangered Species Program
4401 N. Fairfax Drive, Room 420
Arlington, VA 22203
http://www.fws.gov/endangered/

Chief, Division of Conservation and Classification: Nicole Alt, 703-358-2171

Chief, Division of Consultation, HCPs, Recovery, and State Grants: Rick Sayers; 703-358-2171

Acting Chief, Division of Partnerships and Outreach: Jim Serfis; 703-358-2307

Region One — Pacific
Eastside Federal Complex
911 N.E. 11th Avenue
Portland, OR 97232-4181
http://www.fws.gov/pacific/ecoservices/

Chief, Division of Endangered Species: Patrick Sousa; 503-231-6158

States/Territories: California, Hawaii, Idaho, Nevada, Oregon, Washington, American Samoa, Commonwealth of the Northern Mariana Islands, Guam and the Pacific Trust Territories

Region Two — Southwest
500 Gold Avenue, SW
Albuquerque, NM 87102
http://www.fws.gov/southwest/

Chief, Division of Endangered Species: Susan Jacobsen; 505-248-6641

States: Arizona, New Mexico, Oklahoma, and Texas

Region Three —Great Lakes, Big Rivers
Bishop Henry Whipple Federal Building
One Federal Drive
Ft. Snelling, MN 55111-4056
http://www.fws.gov/midwest/endangered/

Chief, Division of Endangered Species: T.J. Miller; 612-713-5334

States: Illinois, Indiana, Iowa, Ohio, Michigan, Minnesota, Missouri, and Wisconsin

Region Four — Southeast
1875 Century Boulevard
Atlanta, GA 30345
http://www.fws.gov/southeast/es/

Assistant Regional Director for Ecological Services
Patrick Leonard; 404-679-7085

States/Territories: Alabama, Arkansas, Florida, Georgia, Kentucky, Louisiana, Mississippi, North Carolina, South Carolina, Tennessee, Puerto Rico, and the U.S. Virgin Islands

Region Five — Northeast
300 Westgate Center Drive
Hadley, MA 01035-9589
http://www.fws.gov/northeast/endangered/

Chief, Division of Endangered Species: Marty Miller; 413-253-8615

States: Connecticut, Delaware, Maine, Maryland, Massachusetts, New Hampshire, New Jersey, New York, Pennsylvania, Rhode Island, Vermont, Virginia, and West Virginia

Region Six — Mountain Prairie
134 Union Boulevard, Suite 650
Lakewood, CO 80228
http://www.fws.gov/mountain-prairie/endspp

Chief, Division of Endangered Species: Bridget Fahey; 303-236-4258

States: Colorado, Kansas, Montana, Nebraska, North Dakota, South Dakota, Utah, and Wyoming

Region Seven — Alaska
1011 E. Tudor Road
Anchorage, AK 99503-6199
http://alaska.fws.gov/fisheries/endangered/

Regional Endangered Species Coordinator: Sonja Jahrsdoerfer, 907/786-3323

State: Alaska

Region 8 — California and Nevada
2800 Cottage Way, Suite W2606
Sacramento, CA 95825
http://www.fws.gov/cno/

Assistant Regional Director for Ecological Services
Mike Fris; 916-414-6464

States: Californa, Nevada

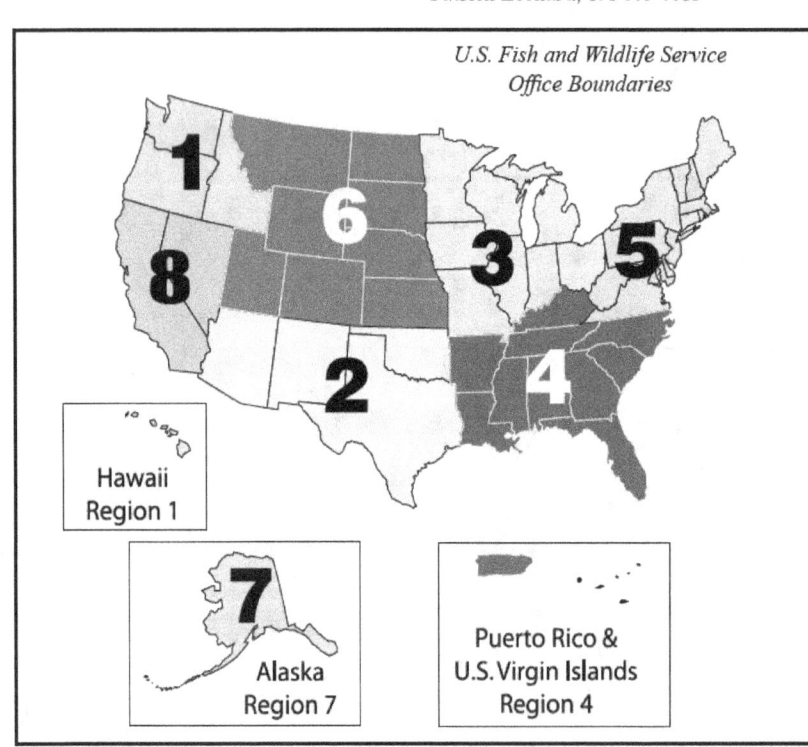

U.S. Fish and Wildlife Service Office Boundaries

Hawaii
Region 1

Alaska
Region 7

Puerto Rico &
U.S. Virgin Islands
Region 4

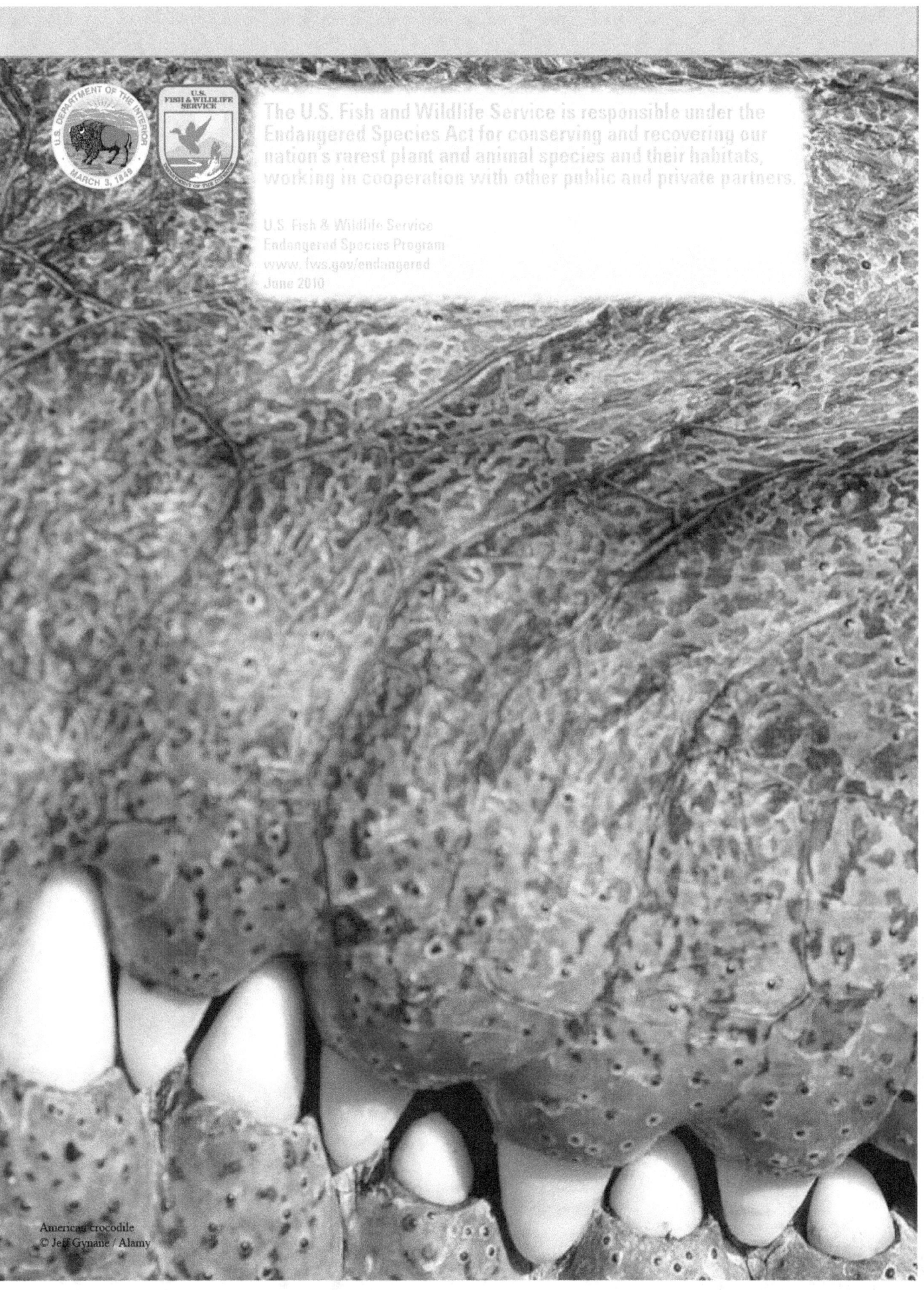

The U.S. Fish and Wildlife Service is responsible under the Endangered Species Act for conserving and recovering our nation's rarest plant and animal species and their habitats, working in cooperation with other public and private partners.

U.S. Fish & Wildlife Service
Endangered Species Program
www.fws.gov/endangered
June 2010

American crocodile
© Jeff Gynane / Alamy

www.ingramcontent.com/pod-product-compliance
Lightning Source LLC
Chambersburg PA
CBHW081116280526

45787CB00007B/2858